BUCKRAMMER'S
TALES

THE CONTINUING *Catboat Summers* ADVENTURES

THE CATBOAT ASSOCIATION, INC.
A Non-profit, Charitable, Tax-exempt Organization

JOHN E. CONWAY

authorHOUSE®

AuthorHouse™ LLC
1663 Liberty Drive
Bloomington, IN 47403
www.authorhouse.com
Phone: 1-800-839-8640

Published by AuthorHouse   04/10/2014

ISBN: 978-1-4969-0045-6 (sc)
ISBN: 978-1-4969-0101-9 (e)

Library of Congress Control Number: 2014906096

To the Conway kids . . .

Abigail, Ned and Caroline

. . . for tolerating my proclivity to stitch *truths* together with excessive amounts of *yarn*.

CONTENTS

PREFACE

In the Fall of 2003, *Catboat Summers*, our modest collection of boating memoirs hit bookseller's shelves. Much to our surprise and delight it quickly became a bestseller among nautical books of this nature; praised by reviewers and readers alike.

This new compilation continues in the same mold . . . Why tinker with success? (Well, actually we have tinkered a tad to select tales with a bit more edge and a touch less maudlin.)

It covers the period from approximately 2003 through 2011 . . . a remarkable time for the Conway family as our kids grew ever bigger and smarter, entered and graduated from college and found their respective places in the real world. My wife, Chris and I also grew during these times . . . sometimes a little too creakily and/or sideways for our liking.

Throughout, our old catboat, ***Buckrammer***, continued to serve as a trusty platform for experiencing many of the joys of summers in our beloved Westport, Massachusetts.

As in *Catboat Summers* we've tried to pace most of these stories so that each can be read "one shot." In an impatient world, many of our past readers relished the ability to enjoy the beginning, middle and end of a story in one sitting.

Finally I wish to thank the good people of the Catboat Association (www. catboats.org) for their support and encouragement. It is through their laudable **Catboat Association Press** that this little volume now reaches you. If you *have* owned, *now* own or *plan* to own or *sail* a catboat, you owe it to yourself to become a CBA member.

Meanwhile . . . If you favor ghost stories, near disasters, family boating misadventures and/or tales of buried treasure, you will absolutely find something to your liking in:

***Buckrammer's** Tales.*

John E. Conway
Westport Point
April, 2014

PHOTO ON THE COVER

I am indebted to Dr. Lawrence (Larry) Borges. MD for the cover photo of **Buckrammer** at Slaight's Dock, Westport Point, Massachusetts.

This is the latest is a series of representations of this scene; a combination seascape and landscape that has become a virtual motif in the 20 years that we Conways have served as caretakers of our historic catboat. Numerous artists have captured the motif and it has appeared as high-end photographs, oil and watercolor paintings, as mirror headers, drink coasters, napkins, ceramic trivets and even clock faces. Who would have thought?

As far as we know, renowned nature photographer and Westport native, Paul Rezendes (www. paulrezende.com) was the first to conceive and capture this picture.

It came to our attention at the February 2003 annual meeting of the Catboat Association. That year the event was held at the Hyatt Regency Newport hotel on Goat Island, Rhode Island. A number of CBA members staying at the hotel noticed a catboat photograph on page 16 of the Guest Guide located in every room. A few asked if this were **Buckrammer**.

"It sure is! How about that!" I was blown away! Except for the fact that the polarity of the photo was reversed (i.e. left is right and right, left), it was a stunning representation of our boat and her Westport "environs" and we had no idea that it had been created.

(Paul's photograph later appeared in an issue of Cruising World magazine that featured a number of his remarkable seascapes.)

John E. Conway

Since then, and as mentioned above, a flood of artists and photographers have sat patiently on the breakwater across from the boat and captured the scene. Most notable among these has been New Bedford artist and gallery owner, Arthur Moniz. (www.arthurmonizgallery.com)

Needless to say, we've been pleased that our "olde bucket" has received so much artistic attention these past decades and hope we can continue to offer her up as the centerpiece of this popular New England motif.

CHAPTER 1

HAUNTING AT SAKONNET LIGHT

"**A**re we *weely, weely* sleeping over in your pirate ship, Uncle John?"

Grace Perron, my three year old great-niece, with melt-your-heart eyes as big as sand dollars, tugged on my shirttail as I slipped a life jacket over her tow-headed noggin.

"Absolutely," I replied. "Just as long as you'll help us find the treasure."

"TREASURE?" All four Perron kids, Emma, age 9, Jake, age 7, Connor, age 5 and Gracie and their dad, Andy (ageless), suddenly came to attention.

Trapped, I sputtered, "Well, er, sort of. Let's board the pirate ship and I'll fill you all in."

With that, the whole entourage clambered aboard **Buckrammer**, our Westport, Massachusetts-based, 1908-vintage Charles Crosby catboat.

Months before, while visiting the Perron homestead near Portland, Maine, I had promised the gang a first-rate adventure aboard our old floating woodpile. July seemed ages away in the snow-encrusted depths of winter but here we were, ready to cast off from Slaight's Dock, launching site of many a **Buckrammer** adventure. (Great-Aunt Chris and niece, Betsy Perron, had uninvited themselves in favor of a "girl's weekend off.")

1

I started the boat's ancient but reliable English Austin-block diesel, Red Jr., and shouted the order to cast off. Andy and Emma let loose the lines, Jake yanked the gear shift into forward and Gracie, from her perch on my lap at the helm, spun the ship's wheel to port.

"Off and away!"

Our cruise would take us from Westport Harbor out past Horseneck Beach and south and west to Sakonnet Point Light . . . a journey of eight to ten miles or so. Experience with my own kids (now all out of the nest) had taught me that short trips provided the least stressful, most compelling boating escapades for small children. This time, with ten miles of open water from port-to-anchorage, we would be pushing things a tad.

Figure 1.1: Sakonnet Light

"Conway kids" expeditions from years past had revealed the area around Sakonnet Point Light as the perfect site for an extended exploration. The circa-1884 lighthouse, situated at the entrance of the Sakonnet River in Little Compton, Rhode Island, sits atop Little Cormorant Rock and marks a ledge and boulder-strewn reef the size of several football fields bounded by the diminutive East and West Islands. We had learned long ago that our shallow-draft (2-feet board up) catboat could readily tuck herself into one of the many lagoons within the reef and hole up for the night . . . safe from both wind and surf. We had also learned that the shallows and tidal pools of the reef provided a marvelous network of nooks and crannies for snorkeling, wading, splish'n and splash'n in waters that hovered around 80 degrees in mid-summer.

As **Buckrammer** exited the Westport River, I whispered instructions to Vice Captain Gracie. The 3-year old master and commander nodded and then, at the top of her lungs barked, "Hoist the weely, weely big sail, you scallyw . . . scullywi . . . . scul . . . you guys."

First mate Andy and his three AB's grabbed the throat and peak halyards, yanked hand over hand on the manila lines and gradually lifted ~750 square feet of canvas into the embrace of a catboat-perfect, 10 knot northwesterly. Magic!

Less than two sailing-filled hours later, **Buckrammer** and crew found themselves anchored fore and aft for the afternoon and night less than 200 yards to the south and east of the lighthouse in 10 feet of clear, warm Atlantic.

"Hey Uncle John, I do believe that it's sandwich time!"

Connor, parked in the galley and broadcasting his world-famous, ear-to-ear smile, swung a loaf of bread up onto the doghouse roof. Jake quickly joined in and pulled jars of peanut butter and raspberry jam out of the storage racks. Andy gave both boys a fatherly warning about manners but a nano-second later, everyone agreed that the boys had it right . . . . lunch!

While the Perrons munched on PB&J's and slurped cold drinks, I reorganized the food stores. **Buckrammer** tradition has it that each crewmember can select his or her meal plan for the duration of the cruise. As a result, the larder contained an eclectic mix of items including (but not limited to) frozen (and rapidly defrosting) French toast sticks, macaroni and cheese, Fenway Franks, chocolate milk, a variety pack of Kellogg's sweetest cereals, nectarines, pancake mix, blueberries, potato chips, orange soda, mini-snickers, cranberry juice, red seedless grapes, sea clams (bait) and powdered sugar donuts. Yum!

After everyone finished their sandwiches and drinks and we had cleaned things up, the wetter aspects of the adventure began in earnest. Andy and

I suggested a loosely defined "buddy system" that would pair Emma with Jake, Grace with Andy and Connor with Uncle John. On our journey from Westport we had towed our little pram, the Splinter, behind the mothership. Splinter would now serve as a shuttle craft carrying buddy team members, in several trips, from the **Buckrammer** over to the shallows and beaches near West Island.

Emma and Jake, both experienced snorkelers, slipped on swim fins and dive masks and began to explore the knee-deep tide pools. Connor and I decided to wade around and look for starfish and shells. Gracie reclined across Splinter's transom seat while Andy rowed her from one rock outcropping to another, both keeping a watchful eye over all. In this way the whole troop spent a diverting July afternoon without a care in the world.

Around four o'clock Andy announced that he and Grace had had enough fun for a while and asked if anyone wanted to join them for a ride back to **Buckrammer**. Conner, his baggy swimsuit pockets jammed to capacity with ocean schtuff, said he would accept the offer. Emma and Jake, the underwater explorers, had managed to swim out of sight towards a cave on the front side of West Island. I volunteered to round up the budding Jacques Cousteaus while Andy dropped off the first Splinterful.

"Emma! Jake!" Sloshing my way around the island, I called out to the kids but they did not reply. "Emma! Jake!" "Hmmmm," I figured, "The little buggers must be in the cave and out of earshot." I'd have to take a little swim myself to work around to the front side. Sure enough, as I breast-stroked my way along, I could hear the older Perron kids talking, faintly at first, then louder, from within the cave.

"What is your name?" (That voice clearly belonged to Jake.) "Why are you wearing a dress, you're going to ruin it." (Emma . . . a dress!?). "Where is your boat?" (Jake) "Are you lost or something?" (Emma).

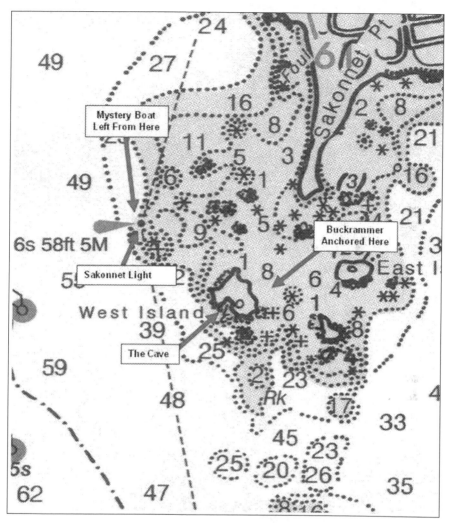

Figure 1.2: Chart of the Haunting Scene

A bit bewildered by the kid's dialog, I paused, treading water, and called out again to them once more. This time they responded almost immediately by dashing out from the cave's mouth.

"Uncle John, Uncle John," Emma breathlessly cried out. "There's a little girl over here in the cave and I think she's lost. Can you come and help her?"

Jake bounded out as well. "Yah, Uncle John, she's so scared she can't talk. Maybe you can get her to."

I quickly switched from goofy uncle into concerned parent and raced over to the cave with Emma and Jake close behind.

The cave opening measured roughly 10 feet by 10 feet and penetrated only 8 feet into the ledge. At this state of the tide, water filled the cave floor to a depth of one foot or so. The kids caught up with me and we looked inside.

Empty!

Emma, Jake and I exchanged double-takes. Huh? We entered the cave but found no one home.

"Maybe she swam around the other side?" Emma reasoned. So we all waded and swam to the left of the cave up towards the lighthouse. Nothing! Puzzled, we looked at one another and turned around to head back to the cave.

"Hey everyone, what's up?" Andy had silently rowed up behind us and, in our sensitized state, nearly scared us to death.

"Jeeeese don't do that!, I yelped. "What? What?," Andy asked. *"What?"*

We all climbed aboard Splinter and explained the situation. Hearing the story, Andy also slipped into parental mode and rowed us around the extended ledge area to search for the lost child. Yet after 15 minutes of effort, neither hide nor hair of a lost child could be found. It dawned on me that Emma and Jake had perhaps played a very clever prank on old Uncle John and dad . . . but the scared look in their eyes showed otherwise.

As we rowed back to **Buckrammer**, the kids told their tale.

Over the course of the afternoon, Emma and Jake had snorkeled about the reef and finally ended up at the entrance to the West Island cave. Looking inside they were stunned to see a young girl, (Emma estimates that she was about 8 years old) sitting in waste-deep water, towards the back. Dressed in a white, frilly "party dress" the child was soaked to the bone. When the girl saw the Perrons, she beckoned them to come into the cave. They did, asked her if she were OK and fired a few other questions (the questions

I heard from afar) But the girl just smiled and remained silent. Then I showed up and, in the time it took Emma and Jake to fetch me, the girl had just simply vanished.

Andy suggested that we row the kids back to the catboat, then he and I would come back to search for the child one more time. As we approached **Buckrammer**, a powerboat that had been hidden from behind the north face of the lighthouse, gunned its engines and pulled out. The boat moved away quickly, but we thought that we caught a glimpse of a child dressed in white clothes in the boat's cockpit along with a number of other children and adults. Had the mystery been explained?

Not completely convinced, Andy and I dropped the kids off and decided to search one more time, just for the heck of it. Another half hour of effort came up empty so we threw in the sponge.

"She must have been a member of the family on that cruiser", Andy and I easily convinced ourselves.

As Uncle John and dad prepared a epicurean dinner feast of hot dogs, mac & cheese, and fruit loops, Emma and Jake told and retold their salty tale. It seemed a touch more embellished with each retelling. After dinner we dug out **Buckrammer**'s concertina and squeezed and screeched out a long medley of shanty songs until everyone grew hoarse. The day ended with all aboard counting shooting stars by oil lamp light, thoughts of the "cave kid" drifting further into our mental recesses

EPILOG

A few days later, with the boatload of adventurers safely back home, Betsy Perron, found a curious artifact in Jake's oversized, rear bathing suit pocket while running a load of wash at our beach house. She placed it on the shelf over the dryer and forgot about the curio until breakfast the following day.

The next morning, while the whole gang munched on blueberry pancakes, Betsey went into the laundry room and retrieved the object.

"Where the heck did you find this?" Betsy asked.

Jake, looked at the object and nearly choked on his food.

"Oh yah! I nearly forgot. The little girl in the cave gave that to me as a gift when Emma turned to get Uncle John."

In her slightly trembling hand, Betsy held the small, barnacle-encrusted head of a Victorian-era doll . . . the plaything of a 19th century little girl.

We all stopped eating and pondered the possibilities. "You don't suppose?"

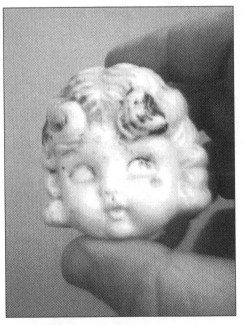

Figure 1.3: The Doll's Head Gift

CHAPTER 2

BIODIESEL BUST

"Shoot the bastard" The handy-talkie crackled. Shoot him!"

The security guards unholstered their weapons. All of the blood drained into my feet and I rapidly turned as green as the environmental quest that had created this mess in the first place.

It all began about 90 minutes before when I decided to buy about 10 gallons of biodiesel on my lunch hour.

Well, now that I think of it, the situation actually traced its roots to the objective of finding a way to take the smell out of diesel fuel . . . a many, many years-long search. You see, the distinctive odor of the stuff gave my better half, Chris (and many other potential catboat passengers), almost instant seasickness. For this reason alone, **Buckrammer** mostly sailed with old men and small children.

Over the years I had tried everything imaginable to eliminate the smell: bleach-rich cleaners, Murphy's Oil Soap (nice smell . . . non-masking, sadly), aromatic cedar blocks (nice smell, ditto on the masking), Witch Hazel and Bay Rum (both super as hair tonics but not as odor-eliminators), dozens of air fresheners (Citrus Magic worked best . . . but not well enough) and buckets of Salty Dog liberally applied to any horizontal or vertical surface (Salty Dog is a blend of pine tar, linseed oil, turpentine and Japan dryer . . . great stuff but, with a distinctive odor all of its own only suitable, as above, for aged males and young folk.) We evaluated all of these . . . and more . . . with the ultimate test of turning the boat's stern to the wind with the engine running. Each and every time the diesel smell, billowing from the exhaust, came roaring back.

We even gave serious thought to repowering the old bucket with a rebuilt Grey Marine gasoline engine. This would require the removal of Red, Jr., our trusty diesel and its controls. It would also mean that we would have to install a number of budget-stretching items such as a new fuel tank, fuel lines and electric bilge-blowers to vent the explosive fumes. (Diesel fumes may stink but, unlike gasoline, they do not explode.)

As we searched for a cure, a miracle of modern science surfaced; Biodiesel.

Made from a wide range of renewable, organic materials (corn, soy beans . . . even old, used cooking oil from French-fry machines), biodiesel (At least the Popular Mechanics article claimed) burnt like diesel but smelled like popcorn popping. Not only that . . . by running one's sailboat auxiliary on biodiesel, one could claim that one operated the greenest of green transportation devices; a plant, wind and sun-powered sailing vessel.

"Eureka!", I yelled aloud. "Gotta get me some of that biodiesel."

All of which brings me back to 90 minutes prior to the firing squad.

The "get" part of biodiesel proved much more challenging than suspected.

An internet search for suppliers revealed (at that time) only one source in New England; Dennis K. Burke, Inc., a family-owned, fuel supply institution located in Chelsea, Massachusetts.

To understand what this meant, you have to understand Chelsea.

The city of Chelsea lies directly across from the City of Boston on the Mystic River. It is the smallest city in Massachusetts in land area but the 26th most densely populated city in the United States. Though kissed by the Mystic River, much of Chelsea lies on an inlet that map makers call the Chelsea River (a sort of tributary of the Mystic), but that everyone in Beantown calls Chelsea Creek.

Chelsea Creek, though located in the innermost of Boston's inner harbor, has water deep enough to accommodate fully laden freighters and oil & gas tankers. In fact, much of the region's ship-delivered produce arrives on "banana boat" freighters that dock here and much of New England's fuel is pumped from a number of fairly impressive tankers that also make "The Creek" their port-of-call. As is the case of most commercial ports, the Chelsea marine terminal area "ain't exactly a purdy place" as one merchant sailor put it. While a lot cleaner than it used to be, "The Creek" is somewhat of an industrial muck-hole surrounded by the trappings of a working waterfront including wildly exotic smells (mostly bad), a significant population of vermin, tumble-down real-estate and a host of unsavory characters.

Thus I suspected that a trip to Chelsea might peg the needle on the religious experience meter but if biodiesel one wanted, that is where one got it.

I placed a call to Burke to confirm that they sold small quantities of the precious liquid. **Buckrammer** has an 18 gallon fuel tank and I thought that two, five-gallon "Jerry" cans of the stuff would suffice for my first trials.

"Yup!", they replied. "We got both 80/20 and 100. What d'ya want?"

"80/20 … 100?" What do you mean?" I asked (as my biodiesel education began)

The patient customer service rep shot back, "80/20 is a blend of 80% diesel fuel and 20% biofuel. We also call it B20. 100 is, you guessed it, 100% bio and also known as B100. Are you gonna use it for your car or for something else?"

I explained what I had in mind.

"Hmmmm. If I were you I'd start with 80/20", she advised. "If that works OK in your boat then you could try 100. Some older engines have had trouble with 100."

I asked what 80/20 smells like.

"Like diesel fuel."

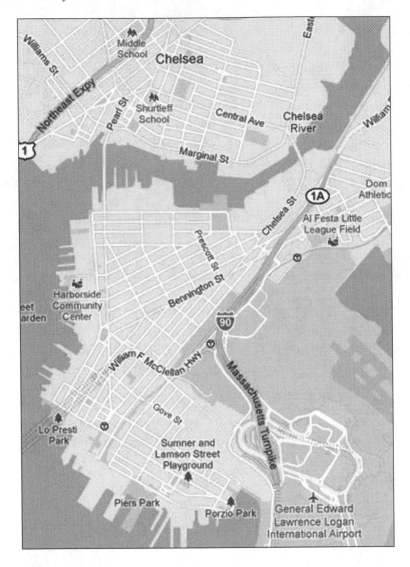

Figure 2.1: The scene of the crime: Logan Airport, Boston and Chelsea, MA
(Source: Google Maps)

"How about 100?", I queried.

"Like nothing . . . hmmm . . . like cooking oil I guess"

"What does it cost a gallon?, I asked.

"At the moment, $2.51 for B20 and $2.97 for B100. And you can pump it yourself right at our terminal."

I thanked her for her help and hung up, somewhat on the proverbial horns of a dilemma.

If I went straight to B100, it might well solve my diesel smell problem but harm the engine. (In fact, it might well solve my diesel-smell problem by *destroying* the engine . . . No diesel engine, no diesel smell, eh!?) On the other hand a switch to B20 would allow me to determine how Red, Jr. responded to a diet of biofuel but would not solve the smell problem.

After wrestling with this for a spell, coward that I am, I decided to go for the B20 and run under that blend for a few weeks. If the engine still ran without incident then I'd add 5 gallons of B100, run the experiment again and repeat this as the fuel tank needed replenishment. Over time (assuming the engine continued to run properly) the system would be converted to 100% B100. Sounded like a plan.

On biofuel-buying day, I tossed two, yellow plastic fuel containers into the back of my car and set course for the Burke brothers establishment. My route would bring me into and through Boston and East Boston on the "open but still under construction", Big Dig portion of the Massachusetts Turnpike. I would then skirt Logan Airport and follow US Route 1A exiting at Chelsea Street.

The trip went without a hitch until I crossed the Chelsea Street Bridge and entered the no-man's land (to me at least) of Chelsea Creek. In those days, before everyone had GPS in their automobiles and smart phones, I had to depend on a book of road maps in order to arrive at 284 Eastern Avenue. On paper the route looked straightforward. In practice, road work associated with the Big Dig created detours into the warehouse district and its maze of small streets and driveways. After a frustrating, traffic-laden adventure or two (F'rinstance . . . While stopped in a line of traffic, I saw lots of rats scurrying around stacked crates of produce. I'm not sure I want to ever eat cantaloupe again), I finally arrived at the biofuel depot about 30 minutes later than planned.

As shown, the Burke Oil facility is massive. I parked my car in a small lot next to what appeared to be their main office and went inside.

A somewhat grizzled gent greeted me from behind the counter.

"Wazup?", he shot.

"Where can I pump B20 biofuel?", I asked.

"Right outside the door you just came in," he snorted. "Pump #3. But youse got to pays up first."

I gave him two $20's and said I needed 10 gallons. He took the bills, examined them and promised to refund the balance once I was finished pumping. With that I headed back outside, took the fuel cans out of my car and headed for #3.

As I walked the 100 feet to the pump, a huge, decrepit garbage truck pulled off of Eastern Avenue and barged towards the pumps, nearly knocking me off my feet.

Through open windows, the driver yelled, "Out of my way, mother f-er"

Stunned, I watched as one of the the fattest, ugliest, filthiest human specimens ever to cross my path hoisted himself (itself?) down from his driver's seat. He looked my way, flipped me the bird and in a quick series of motions unscrewed the cap of the truck's fuel tank and began to pump B20. From the size of the fuel tank and assuming it was nearly empty, I guessed he had about 250 gallons to go. Shahhhhh!

Discretion being the better part of valor, I walked back to my car, put my fuel tanks beside it, climbed in, turned on my radio and waited for toad-man to finish.

No sooner had I done that when one of the biggest BMW's I have ever seen roared in beside me. In the process the "Beemer" managed to thwack one of my Jerry cans.

Out of the vehicle stepped a gold-jewelry-laden greaser.

"Oops! Sorry dude. No harm done."

Figure 2.2: The Dennis K. Burke Fuel Terminal in Chelsea, Massachusetts
(Source: Google Earth)

He picked up the yellow can that he had hit, set it in front of the other one and raced into the Burke building. About two minutes later he flew out of the building, hopped into the Beemer and took off in a squeal of rubber.

About 15 minutes later, toad-man finished filling up, climbed back into the cab and tore off in a cloud of smoke . . . diesel-smelling smoke.

I turned off the radio, got out of my car, locked it up and bent down to grab the fuel cans. It was only then that I noticed that the cap on one of the tanks was missing; the one struck by the BMW. I looked around and spied it lying on the ground a few feet away and totally crushed beyond use. Apparently, the cap dislodged when the can was struck, and somehow rolled under the front tire of the BMW. Arrrrggghhh!

I took the tanks into the Burke building on the off-chance that they might have a spare cap or tank but all I received was a curt "Sorry buddy" from the attendant.

Undaunted, I walked outside and headed to pump #3. A few minutes later, I had 10 gallons of B20 in hand, one sealed tight, the other open to the elements.

I lugged them back to my car and routed around to see what I could scrounge up as a temporary cap. As my family will attest, normally I would have been able to find a solution amongst the "tons" of schtuff that I tend to accumulate in my "ride." Sadly though, under excessive spousal pressure, I had cleaned the vehicle the weekend before and my car was as clean as a whistle. Net: net—No schtuff-based solution to the missing cap presented itself. Arrrrggghhh, again!

Not to be thwarted, I took my cloth handkerchief out of my pocket, stuffed a corner of it into the tank's opening then tied the rest around the stubby neck of the can's spout in a firm, square knot. I figured that this would at least prevent splash-out as I drove back home . . . as long as I took my time and avoided bumps and potholes.

After settling up with Burke rep, I loaded the two tanks into the spaces between the front and back seats, pushed the front seats fully back to secure them, hopped into the driver's seat, closed the door and headed out. Whew! There had to be an easier way to buy bio.

Traffic on Eastern Avenue had increased and this forced me to inch back towards the Chelsea Street bridge, East Boston and the airport. According to the roadmap, it *should have been* a straight shot from the bridge back onto Route 1A and the Pike; Key words . . . should have been. Instead, roadwork blocked the 1A on-ramp and I joined dozens of cars redirected into the bowels of East Boston. From there all detour signs ended and mass confusion reigned. East Boston is a maze of narrow, often one-way streets laid out by historical accident over hundreds of years. Worse, at almost every turn, road work, tree trimming and garbage trucks doing their thing blocked street after street. Without exaggeration, I spent over 45 minutes weaving and dodging throughout the place, often retracing routes traversed just minutes before. Triple arrrgggghhh!

Finally, almost totally exasperated, I turned onto a newly paved, winding road that seemed to lead to the northern end of Logan Airport. I cautiously advanced hoping that this would serve as a "backdoor" entrance to Logan Airport. I figured that once on the airport grounds I could figure my way home fairly easily.

I was almost right.

Turned out, the road *did* lead onto the airport, but through a gated, secure contractor's entrance.

Damn!

As my car and I approached, two husky security guards emerged from the gatehouse and waved me to a stop. I had been doing consulting work at the airport and knew several of the executives there. Best case, I thought, I would ask the guards to call them and, perhaps, they would let me pass. Worst case, I would have to bang a U-turn back into "Eastie."

One guard walked to the right side of my car, the other to the left side.

I rolled down my window.

"Sir, this is a secure area. Unless you have the proper permits and identification, you will have to turn around immediately or you and your vehicle will be found in violation of State and Federal laws," the right guard bellowed.

As I started to explain that I had friends in high places at Massport, the left guard bolted around to my driver's side door and demanded that I "exit the vehicle", place my hands on the roof and part legs. The right guard yanked open the door and, in a twinkling I found myself spread eagle, against my car, being patted down with my wallet removed.

Meanwhile, the left guard radioed that he had a "Code Red" or some such at the Contractor's Gate.

I demanded to know what was going on and was told in no uncertain terms that it was not for me to *ask* questions but merely to *answer* them. I was just about to blow my top when, looking through the back, driver's side window, I had an OH MY GAWD moment.

There, tucked behind the seats were two, yellow fuel tanks, one of them with a white cloth stuffed and tied into the open top, *Molotov Cocktail style.*

OH . . . . MY . . . . GAWD!

Long story short . . . Before the Marines arrived, I was able to convince the guards to call my most senior airport contact. When he heard I was at the gate, without knowing the seriousness of the situation, he jokingly told the guards over their radio, "Shoot the bastard" Shoot him!" Fortunately, a microsecond later, he said "Just kidding."

When the guards explained the circumstances, I do believe that my friend soiled some of his clothing.

After a somewhat lengthy explanation, I was "freed" . . . but not allowed to pass. Thirty minutes later, I found my way to the Sumner Tunnel and headed home to a couple of stiff shots of Ardbeg Uigeadail.

EPILOG

Buckrammer's old engine ran quite well on B20 diesel. In fact, it started more quickly and ran about five degrees cooler with the stuff . . . but . . . the exhaust still smelled of diesel.

The following season I added 5 gallons of B100 to the mix for that year's maiden voyage.

What happened?

Ah . . . That sets the stage for yet another tale. (**Chapter 6**)

CHAPTER 3

PADANARAM DISENGAGEMENT

"**Y**ou know, you've never even asked me once to sail on **Buckrammer**. Am I not loved?"

Nils Bruzelius, former Washington Post and Boston Globe journalist, avid sailor (two-trans-Atlantic crossings) and Westport summer homeowner/turn-up, starred at me above his glasses. We had bumped into one another at the annual silent auction event for the Westport River Watershed Alliance. (www.wrwa.org)

Embarrassed and somewhat flustered I replied, "Nils . . . You know you are welcome to join us anytime and have an open invitation. In fact, Gene Kennedy and I plan to shuttle the olde girl from Westport to Padanarum this Friday morning. Why not join us then?"

"Done! Call on Thursday, remind me and I'll confirm," he quickly replied.

We first met Nils and his family over 20 years ago when the extended Conway family rented their Westport summer house for a few weeks each year over a number of years prior to buying our own cottage there. We had remained friends ever since.

Little did he or I realize what we had both just committed to . . . an adventure not unlike what many sailors have experienced while transiting The Pond.

Friday dawned bright and, as the saying goes, full of promise. Both wind, weather and sea conditions seemed perfect for the 12 mile run from Westport to Padanarum. This was the weekend of the annual Padanaram Rendezvous of the Catboat Association. The event provided an opportunity to gam with a large number of catboat affectionardos and to test our racing skills against catboats of a similar vintage. An early arrival on Friday would guarantee **Buckrammer** a choice mooring in front of Marshall Marine, the event's sponsor.

After Gene and I explained some of the peculiarities of our catboat to Nils (as compared to a more modern, sloop-rigged vessel), we set out under clear skies around 9:00am hoping to be safely moored in Padanaram by noon. My wife Chris would meet us there with her car and shuttle us back to Westport Point for lunch.

We rounded Westport Harbor's Nubble, hoisted the full cut of our gaff-rigged sail, caught the southwesterly breeze (about 10 knots) and headed outward toward Gooseberry Island, our first waypoint.

By the time we reached Gooseberry, the wind had unexpectedly picked up to 15 knots or so and clouds, *heavy clouds*, had begun to move in. The seas remained fairly calm.

Gooseberry Island separates Rhode Island sound from Buzzard's Bay and conditions on the Buzzard's Bay side of the island, where we would soon be located, are typically calmer than on the Rhode Island side. With this in mind we decided to keep all of **Buckrammer**'s sail flying and avoided tying in a trip-delaying reef or two.

The boat flew along at hull speed . . . about 6.5 knots.

We passed Gooseberry but weather and sea conditions continued to deteriorate. The wind, originally blowing from the friendly southwest had shifted more to the south. This put the seas directly on our beam and made for a more bouncy, wet ride. Worse, the sky continued to darken and it soon became evident that we were in for a blow.

Figure 3.1: The day dawned full of promise

(Photo Courtesy Jim O'Connor)

In retrospect we should have shortened sail (i.e. tied in a few reefs) before proceeding. We also should have considered seeking shelter, perhaps in the Slocum River on our port quarter and only a few miles away to the north. But fools that we were and with **Buckrammer** dancing along, we decided it best to press onward to Padanarum, now only 90 minutes or so away at our present pace. Each of us took a turn at the helm to spread the joy.

Nils looked at Gene and I. "You certainly know how to show a sailor a good time" he wryly volunteered.

With amazing rapidity, wind speed increased to about 25 knots and the seas built to an honest four feet or so. The boat was built to handle these conditions but she let us know that she did not enjoy them by throwing a bit of spray our way with an occasional slop of green water over her bow. The three of us donned foul weather jackets and decided to reduce sail.

The design of a catboat, with her mast far forward, shallow draft and large sail, sets up a dynamic wherein she is always trying to turn into the wind. Under normal conditions and with the proper balance of centerboard and sail angle this is hardly noticeable. As wind speed increases however, the catboat tries ever harder to head upwind. To compensate and stay on course, the helmsman angles the rudder a bit off center. The angle at which the catboat's rudder regains control is referred to as the *weather helm* angle. Ultimately, if the wind continues to increase, the rudder reaches a point where it is "hard over" that is, it reaches the limit of its ability to turn. At this point the rudder and steering (either tiller or wheel) is also under enormous pressure. The old-timers used to say that "it feels as if the rudder is dragging the whole ocean behind it." When this happens, the helmsman loses the ability to steer the boat and she heads in an upwind direction of her own choosing . . .

Not good!

With winds now gusting past 25 knots and all of her sail still flying, **Buckrammer** had just about reached this tipping point. (Hmmmm . . . perhaps a poor choice of words)

To maintain control we needed to reduce sail power by reducing sail area.

Rather than risk going on deck to tie in reefs, we decided to use an old trick common to gaff-rigged sailboats called scandalizing. To scandalize a sail you first set (i.e. cleat off) the topping lift (a line that runs from the top of the mast to the end of the main boom and keeps the boom high about the cockpit as the sail is lowered). Then release and slack off the peak halyard, the line the controls the angle of the gaff boom. By slackening this line you can control the "looseness" of the sail. This changes the shape of the sail from an efficient airfoil propelling the boat forward, to a parachute shape that still moves the boat along but much less efficiently. The benefit is that you essentially achieve the same effect as a reef or two by just tightening one line and loosening another all from the safety of the cockpit. The con is that this causes the trailing edge of the sail to flap back and forth (i.e. luff) somewhat violently and noisily . . . a condition that the old salts claim can damage the sail in a relatively short period of time.

Upon scandalizing, the boat quickly regained her composure and her captain and crew their confidence.

Just then the heavens opened.

Gene and I have boated in the rain before but only Nils had experienced sailing under a torrent that simulated an ice-cold waterfall. (We later learned that it rained over 5 inches in less than an hour). Visibility dropped to just a few feet ahead of the boat as sheet after sheet of water poured down. The rain brought one benefit in that it flattened the seas and reduced the rock and roll . . . but boy did it rain. (We also later learned that this rain was associated with a significant and damaging thunderstorm, the core of which passed about 10 miles north of us. Pictures were knocked off walls in homes by the boomers, trees were struck and uprooted . . . real fire and brimstone stuff . . . All not forecast. Fortunately we did not see one flash or hear one boom.)

The downpours continued on and off for about 45 minutes. In between, the seas would rebuild with very wet, breaking waves of about six feet.

Buckrammer barreled forward.

At some point we noticed that the trailing edge of our sail had begun to tear along the stitching. Over the course of 15 minutes or so the tear continued to advance and soon ran the entire length of the sail. The old timers had been correct about the damaging effect of extended scandalizing.

Simultaneously scared and exhilarated, we pressed on and finally arrived at the Dumplings, a nasty collection of rocks about the size of a football field. This waymark signaled **Buckrammer** had reached Apponagansett Bay, the outer approach to Padanaram harbor.

Though the winds howled and the seas and rains saturated us from below and above, the fact that we had made it safely this far caused everyone to break out in broad smiles.

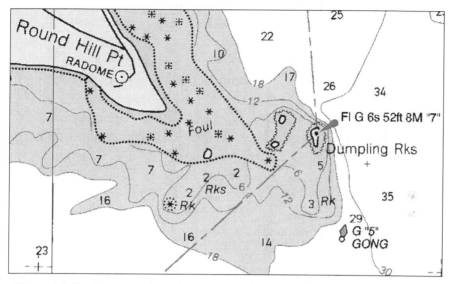

Figure 3.2: Buckrammer almost became part of the nefarious Dumpling Rocks reef.

The approach to Padanarum is strewn with a few, insideous (and often submerged) obstacles with names such as Fatal, Lone, White, Ragged, and Hussey rocks and Bent Ledge among others.

To avoid these we opted to turn at Green Gong Buoy #5 off the Dumplings. This would set us up nicely to follow the remaining aids to navigation directly to the harbor's breakwater. The turn required us to come-about as soon as we passed #5. To guarantee that the boat would do this without stalling (i.e. going into irons) we fired up the diesel and put it into gear.

With Gene at the helm, Nils on the mainsheet and me at the ready, we called out "Ready about" and the wheel was spun hard over.

Buckrammer began to execute the maneuver but just at the inflection point, a terrible rasping noise emerged from inside the helmsman's seat and the boat fell back off without turning. Puzzled, we tried to come about a second time with the same result; the boat refused to come about.

Keep in mind that we still found ourselves in 25+knot winds, 6 foot seas and bursts of icy rain. Further, over the the course of these two, failed attempts to alter our heading, the wind and seas had driven us unnervingly close to the Dumplings. So we had to find a solution and find it fast.

We took the cover off of the steering box to expose the steering mechanism. Manufactured by the Edson Corporation of New Bedford, Massachusetts (Still very much in business since 1859), the gear was, as far as we knew, original to the boat and had served her well since her launch in 1908. We quickly inspected the mechanism and all seemed in order. With the cover off, we attempted a third shot at coming about.

Much to our surprise, just as the boat reached the "about" point, the pinion literally lifted out of the rack and the rudder returned to a center position. We suddenly realized that the force of the wind and seas on the boat during the maneuver was actually twisting the entire vessel enough to lift the steering gear out of contact with the rudder quadrant.

The Dumplings were now just about 150 yards astern.

In the one or two instances when we had had steering problems in the past (due to loosened bolts in the steering box), we had used out little 4 HP outboard as a thruster (it is mounted on a bracket on the transom and always at the ready) and it had steered the boat quite well. Thinking that this might work, we fired up the beast and tried once again to come about using this as our outboard/"virtual" rudder. About halfway through the engine kicked up and we fell back. The force of the water rushing under the boat was actually stronger than the thrust of the engine. This would not work.

The Dumplings were now 100 yards behind us.

Nils, Gene and I looked at one another.

Worst case we needed to anchor ASAP. Otherwise we would be dashed on the Dumplings within the next few minutes. But we all felt that we should first try to bring the sail down to see if that would reduce the forces enough to limit the amount of twist the boat would experience.

Gene took the helm and pointed the boat into the wind. Nils manned the throat and peak halyards and I went on deck to act as the downhaul man.

On my signal we executed the plan. Amazingly, all went well and in record time we had the sail down and secured. With this, Gene threw the helm over once again and the combination of rudder and outboard as thruster, finally, wondrously brought us about within 75 yards of the rocks.

Needless to say, we all exhaled massive sighs of relief.

With the wind at our backs and both the diesel and the outboard set at full throttle, we zoomed the three miles into Padanaram and the Marshall Marine boatyard.

Chris greeted us at the dock. "What kept you guys?"

Our collective burst of laughter nearly knocked her over.

EPILOG

We had lots to discuss at the Padanaram rendezvous that weekend, much of it centered on steering systems. Had anyone experienced anything similar? Is there any way to prevent this? John Brady, master boatbuilder at the Philadelphia Marine Museum, said that he had experienced something similar while delivering Peter Kellogg's newly constructed Silent Maid catboat. But other than suggesting that we somehow needed to" shim the pinion to improve contact with the rack", he was at a loss.

The following Monday I placed a call to the good folks at Edson but they were unable to help. "We stopped making that model in 1922, they reported, "and there sure ain't anyone still here that knows two cents about that system."

However, the engineer in me would not allow this to go unresolved. My experience with **Buckrammer** had time and again shown that the designers and builders of these venerable boats had long ago solved any and all problems associated with these buckets.

So the following weekend I dismantled the entire steering assembly.

Much to my delight, I discovered that a hitherto unknown (to me at least) solution was actually, already in place. Beneath the quadrant but hidden from view (and inaccessable from the current helmsman seat) was a spring-loaded, bronze piston that, properly adjusted, would keep the pinion engaged with the rack no matter how much the boat contorted. Its simplicity bespoke the Yankee ingenuity of the engineer who had designed the whole thing so long ago. A simple turn of an adjusting bolt secured by a lock nut was all that was needed. Over 100 years of wear on the piston had kept it from working but there was enough "meat" left on it for another 100 years or more of service.

To allow ready access, I cut a small opening in the steering box just below the steering wheel shaft so that a wrench could easily reach in for any further adjustment. I cut a square of wood on the table saw and screwed it over the hole for protection.

I'd like to think that **Buckrammer** will never again be caught out in a blow like the one we experienced that Friday . . . but it provides comfort to know that the boat's steering system will not disengage should we ever find ourselves in such a pickle.

FYI . . . The automated wind speed system on the Buzzard's Bay tower,

(http://www.ndbc.noaa.gov/station_page.php?station=buzm3), recorded winds of 35 knots with gusts to 45 that day . . . the tower lies about 10 miles to the south of Padanaram. So we probably experienced similar conditions.

Curiously, Nils has yet to ask for another sail aboard **Buckrammer.**

Figure 3.3: Buckrammer's steering gear with new access to adjustment

CHAPTER 4

EAST & WEST ADVENTURES

The 100 square mile watershed of the Westport River defines a significant portion of the western edge of the South Coast of Massachusetts. Divided into two branches, East and West, the river, in the words of the Westport River Watershed Alliance, ". . . *supports an extensive and productive estuarine habitat including over 1,000 acres of saltmarsh vegetation and over 100 acres of eelgrass beds. There are approximately 3,000 acres of shellfish beds, harvested for both commercial and recreational purposes. The major economic shellfish species include bay scallops, quahogs, American oyster and surfclam. The river is one of the few remaining areas in Buzzards Bay to harvest bay scallops. Soft shell clams and blue mussels are also important recreational species.*"

Conditions that make the river ideal for shellfish and seabirds, namely warm shallow waters with sandy/muddy bottoms surrounded by salt marsh, also render the river ideal for catboating. The Westport River *is* catboat country.

When sea conditions "outside" (i.e. open ocean beyond Westport's barrier beach) give rise to unsafe or unpleasant boating, or for times when we just want to keep things simple, the river provides a wonderful place to "mess about."

But that's not to say it's a *boring*, wonderful place . . . as evidenced the following tales.

EAST BRANCH:
AGROUND WITH THE BUBBLY

"**Y**ou're really going to have them open the bridge?" Chris seemed incredulous.

"Yup", I replied.

"And sail the old bucket up to Hix's bridge?" she continued

"Yup again", I confirmed.

"Then count me in. This is my kind of boating."

"You're really sure that you'll join us?," I questioned.

It was Chris' turn to say, "Yup!" "I'll even prepare a great picnic lunch for everyone."

"OK then . . . Done." I concluded hesitantly. "Really?"

This discussion orbited around a long-threatened promise to sail **Buckrammer** up the East Branch of the Westport River . . . a feat never before attempted in the almost 20 years of us owning the old catboat.

Several hurdles had caused the procrastination.

First, you had to arrange for officials from the State of Massachusetts to open the Fontaine drawbridge. (Actually, open it twice . . . as in coming and going) Un-lifted he span offered only 21 feet of clearance and this presented **Buckrammer**'s 32-foot mast with about 11 feet's worth of trouble.

[N.B. Built in 1958 and originally called the Westport River Bridge, the Fontaine bridge was renamed in 1983 for Specialist 4th Class Normand Edward Fontaine, a Westport resident killed in the line of duty in Vietnam. As a State road, it falls under the jurisdiction of the Massachusetts Department of Transportation]

Second, you had to wait for the State of Massachusetts to finish their Fontaine Bridge modernization project . . . four years overdue for completion. (it had just been completed)

Third, you had to navigate every inch of the way very carefully as the East branch channel narrowed to just about the width (12 feet) and depth (2 feet) of **Buckrammer** in numerous places.

Finally, you had to feel really, really good about your ability to jibe as this would be required many, many times along the ten miles or so of serpentine course that ran from the Fontaine bridge to Hix's bridge . . . the terminus of navigable water (except for canoes and kayaks).

In return for these *inconveniences*, the East Branch offers spectacular scenery, (especially in late Fall when the leaves were aflame), sheltered waters and access to the Westport Rivers Vineyard and Winery, vintners of award-winning, red, white and sparkling wines (aka Champagne).

However, as noted, none of the fun could begin without arranging the Fontaine Bridge opening.

A large sign posted on the bridge span warns that mariners with vessels too large to pass through must call the DPW at least 24 hours in advance to arrange for a crew to open the draw. While there is no charge for the service, I dreaded the thought of having to arrange bridge openings with government officials. I assumed (wrongfully it turned out) that this process would be akin to passing an Act of Congress.

A call to the Taunton Office of the DOT proved me totally incorrect.

"No problem at all, Mr. Conway." A cheerful, DOT manager, Mark Cohen, chuckled. "Just tell me the days and times and I'll have a crew there waiting for you."

"We're thinking of doing this on a Saturday and Sunday," I winced. "Do you work weekends?"

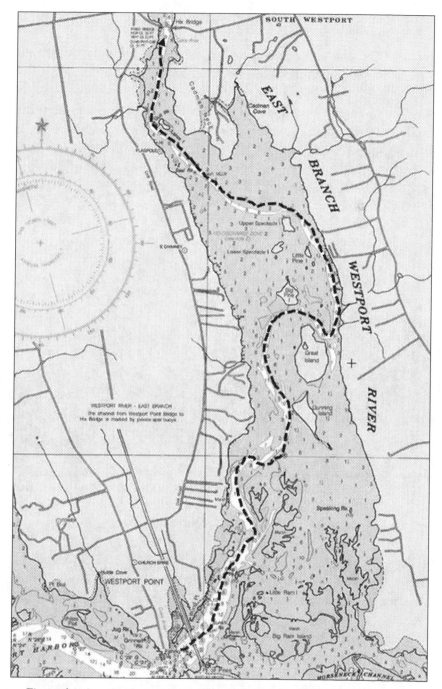

Figure 4.1: A serpentine course ran from the Fontaine Bridge to Hix's Bridge

"No problem," Cohen replied. "We're on call 24 x 7"

Completely flummoxed, I gurgled out the dates and times. Mark confirmed these, I thanked him and our business concluded.

"How about that?", I remember thinking. "A government agency that actually works. Hmmm . . . All to be proved, of course, on opening day, but so far so good."

Figure 4.2: Bompa's Boat and Buckrammer await the bridge opening

The weatherman predicted sunny but cool weather for the weekend in question and Saturday lived up to his forecast . . . a crisp New England Fall day with southwest winds blowing at a near perfect 10 knots or so.

Our East Branch plan had evolved into a multi-step adventure.

1. Ned and I would motor **Buckrammer** through the open bridge at the appointed time and, once on the up-river side, secure her to an available Town mooring.

2. My wife's cousin, Gene Kennedy would then shuttle Chris and Caroline from Slaight's dock in Bompa's Boat, the Kennedy family's center console 18 foot Tripp Angler, named after Gene's late father.

3. The Conway family would then enjoy a pleasant morning sail up the river and anchor at Hix's bridge for lunch.

4. After lunch we'd row to the Hix's bridge landing and hike the 15 minutes or so it would take to reach the Vineyard.

5. After our Winery visit, we'd return to the boat and spend the afternoon sailing in the river's large bay north of the Spectacle Islands.

6. In late afternoon, we'd return to the Hix's bridge landing where Chris and Caroline would rendezvous with Gene for a ride back to our summer cottage.

7. Ned and I would shove off from the landing and find a suitable anchorage downriver to spend a father-son bonding night aboard.

8. In the morning we'd bring **Buckrammer** back to the Fontaine Bridge in time for the second opening.

What could possibly go wrong?

"Hey dad, I don't think she's gonna start" Ned had been cranking the old boat's equally ancient diesel for almost five minutes with nary a sputter. The beast was a notoriously slow-to-start machine in warm weather. The near-freezing temperature of the previous night had chilled its cylinders into non-functional mode.

"OK," I frowned. "Let's try the outboard. I think the diesel has had it for the season"

As a reserve or backup, we always kept a four-stroke Yamaha 4HP outboard at the ready on a transom-mounted bracket and we were constantly surprised that the little thing could push the 5.5 net tons of our old catboat as effectively as it did. A few tugs on the starter rope and one-cylinder wonder fired up.

Just about then the radio crackled "Sailboat! Ya ready?" We looked up at the bridge and saw a crew waving in our direction. I grabbed the mike and said, "Ready as we'll ever be." (I remember thinking "Kudos to Mark Cohen and his dependable DOT operation.")

The bridge sirens sounded and slowly each of the four spans rose into the air. When the spans reached their apex, the lead crewmember waved us onward.

Ned positioned himself in the bow and loosened the mooring rope from **Buckrammer**'s bollard.

"Cast off," I yelled and snapped the outboard's shifter into forward. We were underway.

The current and wind were both heading in the same, upriver direction and with this added boost we literally zoomed through the open draw. The crew gave a little salute as we transited and we returned the same. Within a few minutes we located an unused mooring and tied off. Piece-o-cake!

Gene Kennedy had been shadowing us throughput in the BB.

"You two make it look easy," he laughed. "By the way, welcome to . . . *The Other Side*."

With that it dawned on us that **Buckrammer** was, indeed, finally on the other side of the Fontaine bridge . . . *a first*. Ned came back into the cockpit and slapped me a high five.

As planned, Gene shuttled the ladies and the provisions from Slaight's and before long we had the old bucket's sail unfurled and her course set. Everyone settled into comfortable positions and the journey commenced. The relatively light winds made for easy sailing and no-problem jibes. Ned, Caroline . . . *even Chris* . . . took turns at the helm.

Figure 4.3: Ned at the helm

Chris commented "This is just like sailing on a lake . . . definitely my kind of sailing. We should do this a lot more often." It was not hard for me to agree.

Over the following few hours we passed the five or so islands that hug the channel in this branch of the Westport River. These include Ship Rock, Masquesatch (aka No Name Island), Great, Big and Little Pine and Lower & Upper Spectacle. As expected all were ablaze with colorful foliage.

As we rounded a dog-leg section of channel off of Lower Spectacle, Caroline asked, "What are all of the white things in the trees over there?"

"To my eye," I commented, "It looks like dozens of plastic bags have blown up into the branches. What a shame."

Ned shook his head, "Those aren't bags, dad, there're birds."

Sure enough, as we cruised closer it became apparent that we had stumbled on a massive flock of white herons; hundreds of incredibly beautiful animals roosted in most of the island's trees. Our respective jaws dropped. We speculated that they had stopped on their way south for the winter. Whatever the reason, the spectacle was one to behold.

Shortly before noon we arrived at the anchorage near the Hix's bridge launch ramp and landing.

Caroline postulated, "We simply *must* have champagne with our lunch. Any takers?"

All hands shot up at once and in short order we had rowed ashore and begun the brief walk to the Vineyard.

Founded in 1982, the Westport Rivers Vineyard and Winery began producing their world class products in 1986. As explained by one of the founders, Bill Russell, "We set ourselves up on the sunny, South Coast of Massachusetts. Why? Because we knew, based upon a study of the climate and soils, that this is a wonderful location for growing the kind of wine we love; gloriously aromatic, deliciously crisp wine. And it just so happens that we were right. Our wines display all the world-class characteristics for which we sought. Our soils are dark, rich New England loam on well drained gravel. Our climate is cool but moderated by the warm waters of the gulf stream (which bathes our shoreline all summer and fall). Our rainfall, perfectly accommodating for farming grapes."

Figure 4.4: The Westport Rivers Vineyard and Winery

For today's expedition, the Conway hunting party sought out a few bottles of the winery's Westport Brut, the sparkler that literally put the vineyard on the international wine map . . . and at the market price of $28/bottle, an incredible bargain.

Ned and I were in charge of procuring the bubbly while Chris and Caroline explored the art gallery located in the main house of the vineyard.

Ned reasoned, "I figure one bottle for lunch, one to serve with our dinner and a third for good luck. Sound about right? If you agree, pay the kind lady and I'll pack up things up"

I agreed, even though it meant that once again, Mr. Ned, a master of the artful dodge, be it for gas, food or wine, had stuck me with the bill.

Champagne in hand, we met up with the ladies (no art purchases today) and headed back to the **Buckrammer.**

Back aboard, Chris broke out the victuals . . . and she had outdone herself once again.

"Let's see," she somewhat coyly mumbled while rummaging through the picnic basket, "What have we got? Hmmm . . . Well there's lobster salad in this container, black bean and corn salsa salad in this one, French bread in the basket and chocolate peanut butter cookies in the bag. Anyone hungry?"

Plates were quickly passed around and portions dolloped out. Ned popped open one of the Bruts and handed the bottle to Caroline who lovingly filled our glasses.

Life was good.

Around 2:00pm, after we had cleaned up the lunch things, we hoisted anchor, raised sail and spent a pleasant afternoon lazily cruising back and forth amidst the upper islands and guzzles. As the shadows grew long late in the afternoon, and in keeping with our plans, we headed back to Hix's Bridge landing and disembarked Chris and Caroline to the awaiting care of Gene Kennedy.

"We'll keep an eye out for you guys in the morning back at the Fontaine bridge.," Chris said. "What time are you having it opened again?"

"Eleven o'clock sharp," I replied. "Listen for the bridge sirens and you'll know everything is going according to plan."

Ned and I once again pulled in **Buckrammer**'s anchor and headed downriver, this time on outboard power, to find a quiet spot to re-anchor for the evening.

We decided that a little indent on the northern end of Upper Spectacle island looked like a choice spot and crept the boat in towards the shore there. To prevent a grounding, I kept an eye on the depth sounder and Ned perched himself on the bowsprit on the lookout for hull-damaging rocks. The tide was just about dead low so if we had water under **Buckrammer**'s hull now, it would only deepen as the tide came in.

Thanks to the catboat's incredibly shallow draft (a mere two feet for **Buckrammer** with her centerboard up), we were able to bring the old girl to within five feet of the cobble-strewn beach. Ned lowered and set the bow anchor and I did likewise with a small stern anchor. We like to anchor bow and stern where possible to prevent "turnabouts" should the wind unexpectedly shift while we sleep.

Just as we were getting settled, a voice rang out. "Are you fellas OK?"

Ned and I looked around for the source. "I'm over he-ah on the sho-ah," the voice commented.

About 1000 feet away, on a private dock on opposite shore, stood an elderly gentleman with his hands cupped around his mouth, megaphone style.

"You, OK? Have you run aground? Need help?"

We comforted him by explaining that we were just anchored for the evening and that all was indeed ok.

The man yelled back, "We've never seen a sailboat as big as yours in here. How in Gawd's name did you get under the bridge?"

We explained that we had the DOT open the thing for us but I'm not sure he totally believed us.

"Well . . . OK then," he concluded. "Feel free to tie up at my dock here if you want to."

We thanked him for his kind offer but decided to stay put.

"OK then, G'nite."

Dusk came on us with surprising rapidity as we were moored behind a large stand of white oaks that blocked the twilight. We lit the main oil lamps in the cabin and fired and hitched the old anchor light oil lamp onto the main boom over the engine box (Filled with Citronella oil, the Anchor lamp serves as both our cockpit light and bug repellent)

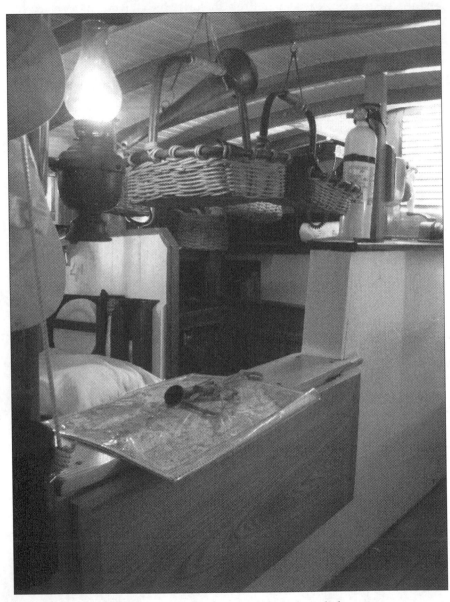

Figure 4.5: Buckrammer's cabin by lamp light

Ned broke out and ignited the gas grill and I dug out the dinner grub . . . which included the makings of a salad, a couple of steaks and a bunch of asparagus. I had even hidden away some rice pudding for dessert. No sense in starving, I thought.

"You break out the champagne, old man, and I'll do the cook'n." Ned offered.

"Works for me" I agreed.

After dinner, Ned revealed that he had snuck aboard a bottle of Ardbeg Uigeadail, one of the smokiest, peatiest, single malt Scotches this side of Edinburgh; a spirit "as deep and mysterious as the loch that gives it its name" and one that smacks of distilled pine tar.

Nectar of the Gods.

Ned had received his Master's degree from the University of St. Andrews in Scotland. Along with his diploma came a newfound appreciation for the "braw usquebaugh" an appreciation that he was slowly educating me in the nature of.

"Care for a dram?", Ned asked. "Aye me laddie," I trilled. "Aye!"

Ned and I sipped a few pours of the magical elixir and gammed well into the night. Topics ranged from Ned's potential engagement to his longtime girlfriend Gabriel (they married a year later) and the joys and challenges of married life to book projects that we were independently working on and Ned's lessons-learned from his two hitches in Iraq as a civilian Defense Department analyst. Sadly, we never got around to solving world hunger. We finally turned-in sometime after midnight and quickly fell into a deep sleep.

"Good Lord, what the Hell was that?" A loud bang woke me with a start. Ned, also awakened by the noise, looked over at me from his bunk. The boat rocked to and fro.

"What time is it?" Ned asked. I squinted at my watch and reported, "5:45 am"

"Bang."

I jumped from my sleeping bag, dashed into the cockpit and was greeted by a brisk 30 knot south east wind accompanied by a stinging rain.

"Bang."

The noise originated towards **Buckrammer**'s bow.

I raced forward. From the bowsprit I could see that the tide was almost dead low and this had revealed a large rock just below the surface. Under normal conditions this boulder would have remained submerged (as it was when we anchored) and close to but well under our stem. However, the wind had kicked up quite a swell and every now and then the boat's up and down bucking caused our vessel to "ground out" on the thing as it was exposed.

Fortunately, the solution was an easy one. I loosened the anchor line by about three feet and the strong, offshore wind quickly blew the boat backwards and out of harm's way.

No damage done.

I returned to the cockpit to find Ned coming up the companionway.

"Wow! This is quite a blow. Was this forecast?," Ned queried.

"Nope!", I replied, "Last I tuned in we were supposed to have chilly but partly cloudy conditions with only moderate winds. Looks like they blew it again, eh?"

Ned nodded. "Ya," Then he added, "Hmmm. I'm wondering . . . Clearly not a sailing day but do you think that our little 4HP horse 'kicker' can push this tub against the blow? What time do we have to be back at the bridge?"

A good part of the blood drained from my face. This *would* be a challenge. It was clearly too cold to even try to start our diesel, so that was eliminated as an option. And the southeast wind would "be in our face" throughout much of the trip from Upper Spectacle to the draw-span.

"Shahhh," I sighed. "This will certainly be interesting but there's only one way to find out if we can do it. So let's get organized and give'er a go, eh?"

"Your boat, dad, your boat," Ned warned.

The time was now just a little after 6:00am. With all of the twists and turns of the river, we had to travel about eight miles from our current location to reach the bridge. It was scheduled to open at 11:00am, so this gave us five hours to move **Buckrammer** from here to there.

"We'll have the outgoing tide in our favor for another hour or two. If we combine that with the thrust from the outboard, we can make bout two knots. We'll have a good shot at pulling this off . . . with about an hour buffer for screw-ups," I calculated.

Ned rolled his eyes but agreed. "Seems reasonable"

We scuttled our planned bacon and egg breakfast (as well as the mimosas we had planned to build by mixing OJ with the leftover sparkling wine from dinner) but we did manage to boil up a pot of strong coffee in our trusty percolator. Ned hauled in the stern anchor and refueled and warmed up the outboard motor. We both changed into dry clothes, donned our foul weather gear and slurped down a few cups of Joe apiece. Ned went forward to haul in the bow anchor and I took the helm. In short order we were off.

Up until now **Buckrammer** "lay to" in the relative shelter of Upper Spectacle. However, as we made our way to the left of the island and into the main channel, we met the full brunt of the gale. The entire boat gave a quiver as we pointed her bow into the tempest. At first, despite our little outboard running at full throttle, **Buckrammer** just sat there, dead in the water with the forces of wind stalemating the forces of outgoing tide and outboard.

"Damn." I whispered.

After sitting is stasis for a minute or two, the old catboat began to move forward almost imperceptibly.

Ned had our mobile GPS unit in his hand, and held it up for both of us to see.

"Half a knot and building, Dad. Wait . . . One knot. One point five. Ahhh . . . One point eight. One point eight. One point eight . . . and holding."

I shot back, "Good enough for now and we may gain a bit more speed as we round the corners and get a boost from the wind for a bit." Ned nodded in agreement.

Sure enough, at the first bend in the river, with our backs now briefly to the wind, the GPS registered almost four knots ground speed. So even though, on average, we cruised along at about half the speed of a person walking, we still had a shot at making our appointment with the bridge.

About halfway into the journey, around 8:00am, the wind and rain picked up to ferocious levels (We later learned that gusts in excess of 50 MPH had been recorded) and our average speed dropped to a hair less than one knot at full throttle. In fact, during some of the more gusty moments, **Buckrammer** actually stopped in her tracks again and shook out a quiver before regaining forward momentum. Worse, the tide was also beginning to slack which meant that within an hour or so it would begin to work against us.

Ned gave me a slap on the back. "Gonna be a close one, eh pops?"

I just gave a very wet wince in reply. At 8:30am the bridge hove into view about three miles distant. I remember thinking, "This is do-able."

As we rounded the bend in the channel near the Gunning Island mud flats, one of the trickiest sections of river, **Buckrammer**'s beam came broadside to the wind.

As if on some demonic cue, one of the strongest gusts slammed us at the worst possible moment, overwhelming both the outboard and the boat.

Within seconds we grounded on the flats and spun stern to the wind. The wind and waves quickly conspired to drive us higher and higher onto the sandbars.

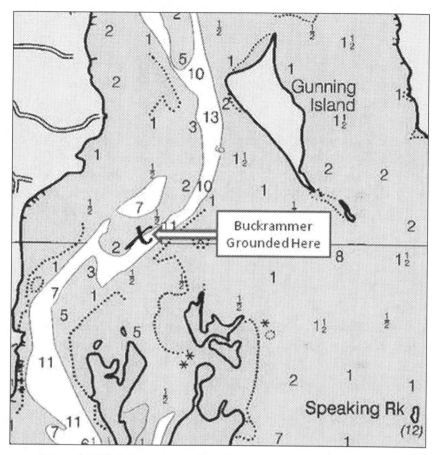

Figure 4.6: We had run aground on the notorious Gunning Island flats

Ned sprang into action and quickly placed the outboard into reverse. This halted our death march onto the flat. I ran forward and raised the centerboard to avoid it being buried, or worse, snapped off at the keel.

These actions stabilized the situation as follows:

1. **Buckrammer** was hard aground in the mud from her bow to amidships. Her stern hung over the drop-off and into the channel.

2. Screaming in full reverse, our little four-horse kicker kept the boat from running further aground but was unable to free us. We were stuck fast.

3. **Buckrammer**'s centerboard was retracted into its trunk and, hopefully, undamaged

4. The tide was dead low but about to turn so, as the saying goes, the incoming tide would, in theory, raise all boats, including ours . . . . given enough time of course.

Ned volunteered to hop overboard and push us off but this would not work. The mud, soft as pudding, would not support the weight of a man and, even if Ned could push us off, the action could leave him stranded on the flat with me short-handed in **Buckrammer** . . . a recipe for a disaster if there ever was one.

I had another idea.

"Let's set a kedge anchor and see if we can pull ourselves off."

Kedging is an old trick often used to pull boats off of a lee shore. A heavy anchor, attached to several hundred feet of strong line, is rowed out as far as possible behind the boat and set. The crew heaves on the line and slowly extracts the boat from its "difficulty."

Ned was a bit skeptical that this would work and, candidly, so was I, but it was the only course of action available with any chance of success relative to our date with the bridge. (In theory we could have just waited for the tide to come in but this would have delayed us for hours and the bridge opening was, by now, about two hours away.)

I climbed into Splinter (Gawd I love that little dinghy) and asked Ned to pass me the storm anchor, a 30-lb Northill affixed to 10 feet of galvanized chain and 300 feet of three-quarter inch nylon anchor line. I hooked the anchor onto one of Splinter's seats and pushed off from **Buckrammer**. Ned would pay out the line as I rowed to the mud bank on the opposite side of the channel.

The wind continued to howl at a good 30+ knots as I rowed into its teeth. The combination of the wind in my face and the tension of the anchor line paying out behind made for one Hell of a hard row. There were a few pulls on the oars when I thought either the oars or the oar locks would fracture but, thankfully, everything held together.

It took almost 15 minutes to reach the opposite shore (only about 200 yards away), I unhooked the anchor, tossed it overboard and backed off, my arm muscles on fire.

"OK Ned," I yelled, "Pull on the anchor line and see if the anchor holds."

My fear was that, in this ridiculously soft mud, the anchor would just slither its way along the bottom without taking hold.

About 200 feet away Ned put tension on the line and gave it a few, powerful yanks.

"Seems to be holding, Dad", he confirmed. "I think we've caught a break."

With that I shot back to **Buckrammer**, secured Splinter and joined Ned at the transom end of the cockpit. The little outboard was still running at full tilt in reverse

Together Ned and I pulled with all of our might on the line. At first it seemed as if we were trying to move the Rock of Gibralter about one foot to the south but slowly, the boat began to move.

"Sonovabitch," I exclaimed. Keep pulling and, oh by the way, get ready to shift the outboard into neutral once we spring free."

"I'm on it," Ned replied.

The Sea Gods must have been with us that day. Though it had taken almost 20 minutes of backbreaking, heaving effort, **Buckrammer** finally sprung free from the muck.

We quickly walked the kedge anchor line from the stern of the boat to the bow and **Buckrammer** whipped around and into the wind. With that I shifted the outboard into forward, took the helm and inched our way to the opposite bank, Ned recovered and coiled the anchor line as we crept along.

When the bow of our boat was almost directly above the Northill anchor, Ned gave it a sharp tug and up she came . . . a mud covered thing of beauty.

"OK dad," Ned yelled. "Get us the Hell out of here."

I threw the wheel hard over, throttled the outboard in to maximum and moved **Buckrammer** once again into the channel and down river.

Time now 9:15 am. Three miles to go and less than two hours to do so.

Ned stored the storm anchor, joined me at the helm and we high-fived.

The wind and rain continued without compassion but we cruised at a more or less steady pace of about 1.8 knots. About a quarter mile away from the bridge, our radio crackled to life.

"This is the bridge-tender hailing the sailboat in transit, do you read?"

"We do," I clicked

"Go to 10," he ordered

"Roger," I replied and switched our radio from the standard in-harbor, Channel 9 monitoring frequency to a working channel 10.

"Are you guys about ready to have us open the span?"

"Just about," I yelled. "Can you see us?"

"That's a roger. We can see you and we will start the process. Out"

We could barely hear the warning sirens above the dim from the wind and rain but howl they did (Chris and Caroline later said they could hear them from our summer place a few miles away) and the spans began their slow climb skyward.

The wind was once again on our beam and this presented one, final challenge.

The opening beneath the span was only about 30 feet wide. With limited forward momentum, **Buckrammer** was more under the control of the gale than the outboard and it caused the boat to crab sideways as we approached.

Ned gave me a look, "Are you thinking what I'm thinking; that we have one shot at this?"

I nodded, my hands firmly on the wheel.

"Yup," "If we miss the opening we'll be blown sideways into the fixed bridge abutments and Gawd knows how we'd get out of that mess. Probably kiss our mast goodbye in the process? So let's not do that, eh?"

"Noted!" Ned agreed.

We aimed for a spot to the left of where logic would dictate, the theory being that the wind would shift our trajectory right as we advanced.

"It's all physics, Ned. It's all physics."

The spans reached their full open positions just as we passed somewhat askew into the opening beneath them. The bridge crew looked down as we passed. A sudden gust hit us while in the opening and Ned had to quickly fend off to keep the boat from slamming broadside into the bridge's pilings.

"We're through!" Ned yelled. "We're through."

I yelled back, "Don't get cocky. We still have to snag our mooring buoy and we'll only get one shot at that as well."

Ned nodded in agreement and, boathook in hand raced forward to the bowsprit. The wind was now at our back and our speed had increased to almost four knots. I put the outboard into reverse as we approached the buoy "hot." It worked . . . a little . . . but we still came into the mooring filed at a good 2 knot clip.

Figure 4.7: Buckrammer, a gale at her back, shoots through the Fontaine bridge

"One shot" buzzed through my head. "One shot."

Ned lowered the boat hook and placed himself at the ready.

In a series of quick moves, he deftly snagged the mooring pennant as it passed and dropped its eye over **Buckrammer**'s forward bollard.

"Secured!", he smiled. "Gawd damn secured."

EPILOG

In record time, Ned and I tidied up **Buckrammer**, stowed everything that needed to be stowed, loaded Splinter with all of the homeward bound schtuff and rowed ashore to Slaight's dock. We tied the Splinter in her usual spot and disembarked.

"I do believe that we have an open bottle of bubbly here, "Ned commented while pulling the partially consumed bottle from our cooler." I think that we need a little celebratory toot."

I agreed. Ned took the first draft, I the second and we passed the bottle back and forth until empty. With that we succumbed to the moment and collapsed on the float; prostrate, face up and dead-man tired.

It was in this position that Chris and Caroline found us . . . and the empty Champagne bottle . . . when they arrived to pick us up.

Chris just shook her head.

"Look at these guys, Caroline, will you? After a great night and an easy morning they decide to get bubbled to the gills. What a pair. What a pair."

John E. Conway

WEST BRANCH:
THE PHANTOMS OF GREAT ISLAND

"Dad, dad . . . for Gawd's sakes, wake up," Caroline pleaded. "Wake up or you'll miss the ghosts."

Aroused from a very deep sleep in a very warm berth it took me a few minutes to reenter reality.

"Huh, wha?" I sputtered and blubbed. "Wha'ya talk'n 'bout? What time is it?"

Caroline crouched on the top rung of the companionway ladder, her hands clenching the wooden slide that supported the doghouse roof

"About 5 o'clock in the morning. Dad . . . Look! I count about six, no, maybe seven ghosts strolling the beach on Great Island," Caroline whispered. "You've gotta see this."

Now more awake than not, I slipped from the cozy covers and crabbed over to my daughter in the companionway.

"See!" "See?" Caroline pointed to the distant shore.

I stuck my head up through the doghouse opening, looked out on the scene *and dropped my jaw*. About 1000 feet away, on the shore of Great Island, a half dozen or more luminous, ethereal figures seemingly strolled along the strand

I could barely mutter an "I'll . . . . be . . . damned."

The adventure had begun a few days earlier. Caroline, needing a break from her State Department duties in DC, decided to spend a late October weekend in Westport. Most of the summer crowd (locally know as "turn-ups" because we "turn up" in the summertime) had left for the season with no idea that Westport in the Fall often proved as the best time of the year.

The few hardcore turn-ups among us knew otherwise and tried to squeeze every drop of summer out of the place until the snow flew.

Cool (sometimes cold) evenings, aka "good sleep'n weather", typically gave way to sultry, dry days that rained buckets of sunshine. This often coaxed 75 or more degrees out of the atmosphere. Not so bad.

This was just such a weekend.

Caroline had originally planned to just sit on the beach and read and maybe bike a mile or two or ten. However, by chance, a scheduling screw-up had postponed **Buckrammer**'s Fall hauling until the first week in November. When Caroline learned that the boat was still in the water, she asked if we might take one, last cruise of the season. It took me about 10 nanoseconds to agree.

Caroline developed a plan.

"I'm thinking that we take a lazy, late-day sail up the West Branch," she suggested. "Anchor off of Judy Island, have a sunset supper there and crash." "Then I'm thinking coffee, blueberry pancakes (with real maple syrup) and bacon in the morning and a leisurely sail back to be home before noon."

"Works for me," I agreed. ("Sounds like heaven," I thought.)

Judy Island holds a special place in the Conway hearts as the destination of our family's first, major boating adventure together. In the summer of 1990 we had just completed construction of our little dinghy, Splinter, and sought "places to go and things to do" on the water. Caroline was 4 and siblings Abby and Ned 10 and 8 years old respectively In studying the charts of the Westport River we identified a sail to Judy Island as the ideal day trip. (Of course we renamed the place Pirate Island for the occasion) Somehow Chris, the kids and I squoze into the diminutive little boat (As Chris put it, "Thirty feet of people in eight feet of boat") and made our way there and back, sometimes sailing, sometimes rowing or pushing and not without a few laughs *and tears* along the way.

Figure 4.8: Splinter, Caroline, Ned and Abby on their first visit to Judy Island

After a stop at Lee's Market for provisioning, we loaded Splinter at Slaight's dock and rowed out to the mooring field and our old catboat. The weather promised to be storybook perfect for the season with clear, star-lit skies (particularly so given Westport's distance from Big City lights), cool temperatures (72 degrees in the evening dropping into the high 30's by midnight then rebounding back into the 60's shortly after sunrise) southwest winds of about 10 knots and modest humidity. Ideal.

The current was running downstream so rather than fire up the noisy engine we decided to let tide and wind work their magic and drift-sailed off the mooring. Caroline and I had done this a hundred times. Without a word between us but working as a coordinated team, we easily had **Buckrammer**'s great wing unfurled and sheeted. A crisp tack to starboard had the old bucket pointing in the right direction and we were off.

"Piece O' Cake, eh, Dad?"

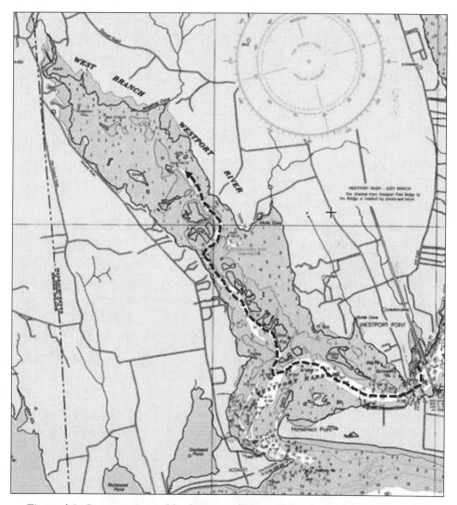

Figure 4.9: Our course would take us up the West Branch of the Westport River

Our course would take us past the Town Fishing Docks down river to the tidal flat we call the Jumping Sandbar. There we would enter the Canoe Rock channel and hang a right towards Ed Carey's boatyard. Once past "Club Ed" a quick starboard tack followed by an even quicker port tack would position us for a straight shot to Judy Island with the southwesterly at our backs.

All went according to plan and less than an hour after casting off, **Buckrammer** and friends were safely anchored for the evening. The air and water temperatures were warm enough for a pre-supper swim and Caroline and I took turns cannon-balling off of our boat's bowsprit, climbing up **Buckrammer**'s rudder steps and repeating the process a few dozen times.

While still in our bathing suits, Caroline suggested that we might pay "Pirate Island" a return visit.

"I wonder," Caroline mused, "I wonder if the old duck blinds are still there?"

"Only one way to find out," I offered.

We climbed into Splinter and rowed the few hundred feet that separated our boat from the island.

Almost ten years had elapsed since our last visit and we weren't quite sure what we would find. In earlier times the island offered an abundance of kid-friendly amusements ranging from the remains of sea and air creatures (e.g. the dried carcass of the largest horseshoe crab we have found to date and numerous seagull skeletons, sea and snail shells, etc.) to the aforementioned duck blinds typically peppered with the brass shell casings of hundreds and hundreds of spent rounds

As we ran aground on the shallows of the marsh, Caroline jumped out, beached the dinghy and secured the boat's anchor into the rocky sand.

We spent a diverting hour exploring this football field-sized "atol" and confirmed that, as Caroline so succinctly put it, "Nothing has changed."

Back aboard **Buckrammer** we slipped into dry clothes. With a dewy dusk approaching, I built a robust wood fire in our old Shipmate stove (not cold enough for the blast-furnace level of heating provided by a coal fire) and prepared our dinner victuals. Tonight's menu would celebrate a classic Yankee Saturday night supper tradition by serving up skillet-fried ham steaks, Boston Baked Beans and steamed brown bread. Unlike our Puritan forebears, however, we'd wash all of this down by sharing a nice bottle of Mark West Pinot Noir between us.

To use the tired but appropriate cliché, ham and beans were just what the doctor ordered to chase away the chill of an October evening. This coupled with the heat thrown off by our oil lamps and the glowing embers in the stove made for a very comfortable below-decks retreat.

After cleaning up the dinner things, Caroline and I retired to our respective bunks and read ourselves into the Land of Nod all the while coddled by the gentle rocking of the old bucket. Ahhhhh!

"Come on dad,. Get dressed. We've got to check this out," Caroline had her foul weather pants on and was half way into the dinghy before I realized what she had in mind.

"Are you kidding?", I sputtered. "You can't want to row over to those things."

Caroline just shot back one of her famous laser-beam looks and I knew she meant business.

"Well, if you're too much of a coward, then I'll just row myself." She challenged.

Actually I *was* a bit of a coward when it came to such actions as dancing with the Devil (or Devils). But I couldn't let Caroline go it alone.

"OK! OK. Hold your horses and give me a second to put on my rain gear."

In short order we shoved off in Splinter from **Buckrammer** and headed towards the wispy, semi-luminous creatures still very much in evidence on the distant shore of Great Island. A heavy dew had fallen and as had the temperature but the foul weather clothes we wore protected us from the damp as well as the cold. Nevertheless, a chill of a different stripe slowly crept down my spine as we neared the island and it's spectral residents.

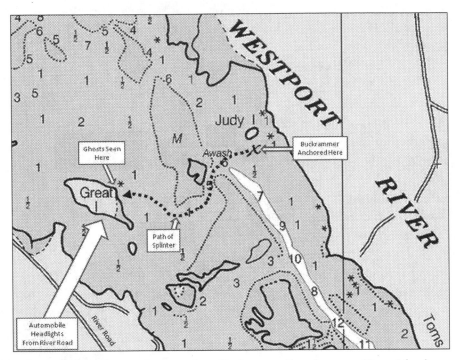

Figure 4.10: It was a short row from Buckrammer's anchorage to Great Island

Caroline acted as the coxswain and directed my efforts as oarsman.

Enroute, Caroline whispered . . . "Dad, isn't this the island where that religious cult operated?"

I reminded her that it was. "A I recall it, the Westport Historical Society interviewed an old time resident, name of W.F. Wyatt. They published his or her comments about the place and the group of religious pilgrims who lived there." Wyatt's tale went something like this . . ."

*The group, called **The Mission of the Holy Spirit** but known locally as the **Holy Rollers,** was not well understood. In the early 1920's they established a small colony near Adamsville R. I. on River Road in Westport and on Great Island opposite. The group supposedly existed for the sole purpose of providing an environment of calm and serenity for unwed, expectant mothers during their maternity.*

They built prominent buildings on both the land and island for the purpose.

In return for five years of their time and good will, during which time members were housed, fed, clothed and otherwise provided for, the mothers were guaranteed to be freed from work for the rest of their lives. Real estate holdings in booming Fall River would sustain all in comfort.

However in 1925, greed and jealousy (of one family in particular) triggered a revolt amongst the small group. Sensing the on-coming treason, the founder and self-styled Holy Ghost Himself, Eugene Richer, quietly left with a few close followers.

Soon thereafter, a scandal erupted.

Some Fall River men residing in the eastern section of the city somehow lost considerable money through the operation of the colony. It was on their complaints that the police were brought in. One Adelard Giasson, known as The Apostle, was arrested on a charge of conspiracy and the place was essentially mothballed.

I continued, "At some point a suspicious, major fire destroyed the complex on the island. All that remained to this day of that complex were the poison-ivy-encrusted building foundations along with the concrete pilings and footings of the boat docks on the island's west side beach. The mainland buildings still survived as a private residence."

Caroline pondered this for a few seconds and said. "Hmmm. With that curious history there's no telling who or what might be haunting those grounds. Did anyone die there? Maybe more importantly, is anyone buried there?"

"Beats me," I replied.

We had now rowed about half way to the island. The whispy figures continued their "danse macabre" and became ever more distinct.

We paused to study the situation.

"Geeze, they do look like ghosts. This is amazing," Caroline commented. "Whatdaya think?"

"I don't know . . . but if they are actual ghosts, based on their location they might be the wrong kind." I replied

"Huh?" Caroline asked.

"Let me explain," I offered. "As you know, in the late 1970's your mother and I were editors for a Boston-based electronics magazine, EDN." "One year, I think it was 1976, the Institute of Electronic and Electrical Engineers held their annual convention near our offices and your mother and I were assigned to attend. Most of the sessions were boring to the point of tears. One, however, on the topic of Psychotronics, captured everyone's interest." The IEEE had formed this new group charged with the mission of determining if ghostly phenomena were electrical in nature. Experts from Duke and other prominent universities presented Psychotronics-related papers.

During this session a panel summarized the findings-to-date. They concluded:

1. Ghosts were indeed electrical phenomena of some kind
2. Ghosts could be separated into two types; *Projections* or *Disembodied Intelligences*

"As I recall," I continued, "Projections or projected ghosts represented the majority of the cases. They were merely (merely!?) air-borne images somehow electrically-generated unconsciously by person endowed with this ability. Phenomena ranging from glowing mists, spirit lights, luminous balls and such to actual images of people were all ascribed to projection. Further, the person projecting the ghostly "auras" needed to be in close proximity to them. As far as the scientists could determine, no one was able to project beyond 10 feet or so. So only those persons close to the source of the projector would experience the haunting. Thus, except for scaring the bejeebers out of everyone, projections were considered as harmless as your shadow.

"Disembodied Intelligences (DI's) were something entirely different. The experts postulated that these were actually a form of intelligent life separate from that of human kind. While extremely rare, they did really exist (!) and could interact directly with our physical world. The more common term for these beings was "poltergeists" derived from the German words *poltern* ("to make noise") and geist ("ghost"), ergo "noisy ghost." "For reasons unknown, the experts explained, most of these creatures tended to make mischief. This could range from the classic door openings/closings, lights being turned on and off and similar antics to actual physical harm. In one case presented at the conference, the DI physically tossed its victim across the room and broke her arms. The panel concluded that human-kind should make every effort to avoid contact with DI's. They were the "wrong ghosts" to mess around with."

I concluded, "So, I'm thinking that since there are no people on Great Island to project images, these must be DI's . . . assuming that they are really ghosts of course."

Most of the color had drained from Caroline's face.

"Geez dad . . . Just the important science lesson I needed right now. NOT! How about we turn around and head back to the boat?"

I could not resist, "Well, if you're too much of a coward, then I'll just row myself."

With this we both had a good laugh.

"OK! I'll continue on with you," Caroline said cautiously, "But at the first sign of anything physical we're out of there."

"Agreed!", I nodded.

It only took about five minutes or so more to complete our row to the island.

For our landing, we chose a spot a few hundred yards south of the apparitions.

"Hey dad," "You go first."

I put my hands on my shoulders and flapped my arms in a little chicken dance. Caroline poked me in the side.

"Just go," she said.

We slowly walked north and soon stood face-to-face with the closest phantom. It consisted on a column of foggy mist that just wavered back and forth in the still, clammy air.

I reached my hand into the thing and the temperature in my fingers and palm fell about ten degrees.

Nothing else happened.

Emboldened by my non-event, Caroline walked over to the next column in the chain and gave it a probe with her outstretched hand and arm.

Aside from the same chilling experience, nothing happened.

"Sorry to disappoint you PD, but I think this is just some weird form of fog or mist."

She agreed. "Actually this is pretty cool," she added. "Tell you what. I'm going to step right into the column and see what happens." She added with a smirk, "If I disappear forever, tell everyone I loved them."

With this she leaned forward and became one with the second "spirit."

Almost instantaneously the mist dissipated but not before Caroline released a big yell.

"Jiminy Christmas. That was freezing. What an experience Dad, you've gotta try this"

What the Hell, I thought and stepped into the spectral breech.

"Whoa!"

It felt something akin to taking a cold shower . . . and shivers literally shot down my spine . . . a most odd experience.

Then, much in the same manner as Caroline's "ghost", my foggy phenomenon quickly evaporated as well.

By now, daylight had started to dawn and Caroline and I were better able view the extended landscape. Virtually the entire northern end of the island was peppered with dozens and dozens of similar fog columns . . . a ghostly army.

Caroline was the first to speak. "This is one of the most strange yet beautiful weather phenomenon's I've ever seen, don't you agree?"

"Absolutely," I chirped. And all thoughts of projected ghosts and disembodied intelligences dissolved as rapidly as our individual mists.

Just then the first rays of sunrise shot out from behind the trees lining the old Southard property to the East. Within seconds, the foggy legions completely faded from view.

Incredible. We both agreed that this was indeed one for the books. (sic)

Somewhat humbled by the experience, Caroline and I walked silently to Splinter and began our row back to the **Buckrammer**.

About ten minutes later we secured the dinghy to the old bucket and climbed aboard.

Caroline was first to break the silence. "How about those pancakes?"

"Coming right up," I smiled.

EPILOG

We spoke with a number of weather experts since our ghostly experience and asked if they could explain what we witnessed. Most think that we encountered some combination of ground fog and columnar sea smoke. Apparently the high humidity coupled with the near freezing temperatures conspired that night to produce conditions perfect for this phenomenon.

However, the more the romantic in me thinks about it the more I feel that we may have encountered yet a third form of specter.

You never can tell.

Figure 4.11: The experts say we saw ground fog and columnar sea smoke

CHAPTER 5

THE BARNSTABLE HARBOR EXPEDITION

"I'll do my best to be there. Promise!"

I could imagine Tim Coggeshall smiling on the other end of the phone.

"OK John, we'll be counting on you." Tim replied as we both hung up.

With that I had committed **Buckrammer** to serve as the "Queen of the Fleet" for the 100th anniversary of the Barnstable Yacht Club.

I remember thinking, "Well . . . I've got about seven months to plan for this. No prob."

From 1938 to 1954 our old catboat, then known as Pelican, called Cape Cod's Barnstable Harbor her home port and all seven Coggeshalls her family (mother and father, Ester and Jim and their children, Wells, Tim, Clark and Sarah)

After countless adventures and misadventures involving Pelican, the Coggeshalls and most of the BYC's members, the club had unofficially adopted the old boat as its pseudo mascot.

So it only seemed fitting that she should return for the centennial event . . . assuming she remained fit enough to navigate and survive the 300+ mile round trip up the notorious Buzzards Bay, through the Cape Cod

Canal into Cape Cod Bay then through the sand-bar-riddled Barnstable Harbor . . . and back again.

Needless to say, the months passed in a blink and we suddenly found ourselves smack dab against the event deadline.

My outbound "float plan" contained two legs: The first would bring us from **Buckrammer**'s Westport home to Onset Bay in Wareham; The second through the Canal and then along the Sandwich shore and into Barnstable Harbor. With the right weather and tides (and a little luck) this could be accomplished in two days of leisurely sailing. We'd spend a day or two at the celebration (participating as the lead vessel in the Parade of Boats) then retrace our steps on the return trip.

Sadly, the appointed dates for the trip coincided with my kid's summer camp and jobs schedules, Chris's volunteer missions and a whole host of other distractions for my friends, so I would have to make the first leg and a half of the trip flying solo.

Happily, on the "third half" of the adventure a collection of Coggeshalls would rendezvous with us at the marina located in the East end of the Canal. We would then sail together to the BYC where a prime mooring awaited.

I spent the week prior to the trip provisioning **Buckrammer** for the journey ahead. This way I could put in a half days' work at my office then simply jump in and go around noon on the event weekend's Friday.

Friday, July 7th dawned with spectacular weather and sea conditions predicted for the following ten days . . . a summer miracle of sorts.

If only my prediction of a half day's worth of work had followed suit.

One of my most important clients insisted that we "put in a little extra effort." to finish a phase of a project ahead of schedule. As a result, my noon departure turned into a 4:00pm exit right into the teeth of a Boston-in-the-summer traffic jam. Net: net, I got to the boat around 6:30pm debating with myself whether I was up for a little night sailing. Under the best conditions I would not make Onset Bay until 11:00pm or so . . . well into the dark of of a July summer evening.

Figure 5-1: Buckrammer left Westport on a perfect Summer afternoon

"Dad, you are such a wimp." My son Ned could not believe that I hesitated.

He had spent a semester at sea aboard the square-rigged training ship Corwith Kramer in mid-Atlantic and had grown to love night sailing. I had little, actually no, experience in this black art.

"You'll LOVE it", he prodded. "Piece-O-Cake." "What could possibly go wrong?"

"Hmmmm," I cogitated. "Alright, I'll give it a try. But If I die I'll never take your advice again."

"Deal," Ned shot back. "Deal."

(To be honest, my real worry centered on what sea conditions I would find off of the infamous Stoney Point Dike near the approach to Onset Bay. I had almost lost a boat there once before in the mile-long, ten-foot standing wave that often forms in this Devilish place. I shuddered to think what "shooting the curl" might be like at night. The good news was that if I were able to pass by the Dike before 11:00pm, sea and tide conditions would not be conducive to standing wave formation.)

Night fell about half way to Onset. To speed things along, I had motor-sailed most of the distance thus far. From here on in, however, I would motor only. It was hard enough to single-hand **Buckrammer**'s ~750+ square feet of sail in daylight. I was not about to tempt the Gods trying to manage that canvas and rigging all along at night. (I *am* a wimp)

As a part of my planning I had entered a series of way points into my primitive but effective, handheld GPS unit. As the darkness descended I would become more and more dependent on this amazing gadget to point me in the right direction.

Before long I came to appreciate Ned's advice. Away for the distracting lights ashore, the clear sky blazed with uncountable stars. The Milky Way emerged as I had never before seen it. The spectacle was jaw-droppingly beautiful.

Almost as beautiful but more problematic were the hundreds of navigation lights that marked both the channels *and hazards* of the Bay. Buzzards Bay is one of the most populated and traveled waterways on the Eastern seaboard. Hundreds of vessels from ten foot sailing dinghys to Queen Mary-scale liners ply these waters daily. To assure safe passage for this diverse fleet, the US Government has placed an equally large number of aids to navigation throughout. In daylight, these buoys and markers are easy to locate and position by eye.

At night, however, due to the loss of perspective, it becomes much more difficult to determine how close or far away the lights atop the buoys are relative to your existing position. If one were navigating in a less densely marked area, a simple glance at a nautical chart would reveal the light's position. However, Buzzards Bay at night displays so many "points of light" that it becomes almost impossible for an untrained eye to easily determine if the flashing red, green or white light to port was 500 feet away or 5000 and how it was positioned relative to the dozens of other flashing lights in the field of view.

(To be fair, most navigation lights, be they simple buoys or historic lighthouses, blink in a unique, identifying sequence, not unlike a Morse Code of sorts. Each of these blink patterns is written next to the navigation aid's icon on the nautical charts. So, in theory, all you have to do to identify the position of a nav-light is observe the blink pattern then find its match on your chart . . . an almost impossible task when underway, solo in a small boat bouncing along in three foot seas surrounded by hundreds of near and far blinking lights.)

I decided to give up (mostly) on the lights and came to depend on the GPS.

Modest but continuous head winds and currents conspired to slow my progress. By 10:30pm it became clear that I would not reach the Stoney Point Dike for another hour or so. To avoid the potential standing wave I could bail out and head into Marion Harbor but this would mess up my plans to easily reach the Eastern Canal entrance rendezvous point on time in the morning. So I decided to press on.

The southern end of the Dike is marked with a very bright white navigation light. I could clearly see the light some distance ahead and headed for it. After a few minutes I noticed that in aiming for the light, my GPS unit suggested that I was heading in the wrong direction. At first I thought that this was an anomaly as the light was clearly visible and that the GPS would self-correct in a minute or so.

However, as the minute passed, the GPS indicated that I was even more off course than before. So what to do? Continue to aim for the navigation light or put my trust in the GPS (which, if wrong, would direct **Buckrammer** towards broken ground east of the Dike.)

I turned off the engine and drifted along silently flipping mental coins heads or tails.

A pilot friend of mine has always cautioned that the first rule of navigating in poor visibility is to "trust your instruments." So, somewhat hesitantly, I restarted the engine and pointed **Buckrammer** into the GPS course.

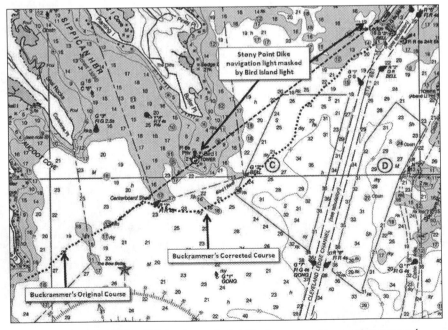

Figure 5-2: Bird Island Light almost fooled **Buckrammer** into running aground

Good thing that I did. About 30 minutes later the real Stoney Point Dike beacon emerged from behind Bird Island and the bright light that I had been following turned out to be an uncharted light operating in the restored, historic Bird Island lighthouse. Had I followed the Bird Island light I would have run aground on the sand flats south of the island.

I'll never again mistrust the instruments (mostly)

Buckrammer arrived at the end of the Dike shortly before midnight. The seas were as flat as the proverbial pancake.

"Ha! We've dodged the bullet," I yelled at the Dike's light tower as we transited. I recall thinking, "Only about five miles to go before we reach Onset."

Just as I finished my boast, a lightning flash winked off of **Buckrammer**'s port quarter. It was followed about 20 seconds later by a distant clap of thunder.

"Hmmm. Divide by 4 rule places this 5 miles away," I calculated.

A few minutes later a second bolt flashed followed by thunder 15 seconds afterward.

"Damn."

I slowed the boat to a crawl, locked the helm and raced below to gather my rain gear.

My return to the cockpit was greeted by another flash, this time off of my starboard side. Thunder followed that flash 12 seconds later,

"Three miles. Double damn."

I later learned that two massive thunderstorms, each generating microburst winds in excess of 60 knots, had formed a few miles to the West and East of the Dike, but, at that moment I believed that I might be heading into the middle of a single, super cell. Expecting the worst, I put the boat into neutral, cinched my life jacket a bit tighter (I always wear a life jacket when single-handing . . . day or night) and battened down the hatches (i.e. Secured anything that could fly away below decks), put the sail cover on the sail and tied the boom with extra lashings.

I put the engine back in gear and set the throttle for full speed ahead. With some luck I might make the safety of Onset Bay before all Hell broke loose.

Thunder and lightning grew ever closer on both sides of the old catboat and I expected gale forces (maybe even near-hurricane force winds) to erupt at any moment but the seas and winds remained eerily calm.

Boat and captain pressed on.

Follow the Light . . . ning

Virtually surrounded by nature's wicked fury but somehow immersed in a bubble of tranquility **Buckrammer** finally reached the buoys that marked the entrance to Onset Bay.

The OB entrance is one of the more interesting nasty little channels to be found in these coastal waters. Small but lethal, semi-submerged piles of granite and bedrock border a 15-foot wide, zig-zag cut. On one side lies the tantalizingly safe waters of Onset Bay on the other the nerve-wracking, fast-flowing waters of the Stoney Point Dike and the land-cut of the Cape Cod Canal.

By day the OB channel is merely difficult, by night . . . well I had never entered Onset Bay at night. Fortunately, my family had owned a summer cottage on Onset Bay for a number of years and I was fairly familiar with and respected this entrance.

I throttled down, grabbed my biggest flashlight and turned the boat into the channel. Small, unlit buoys marked the hazards. The beam of the flashlight hit reflective tape on each buoy and they glowed in the dark. About half-way into the sluice, without warning, the flashlight's bulb blew out.

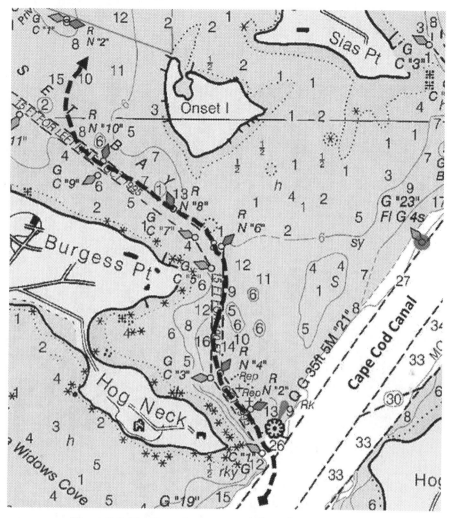

Figure 5-3: The Onset Bay was especially tricky to enter at night

"Arrrrgggghhh"

About to despair, a bolt of lightning flashed, then another. These were followed in rapid succession by many more. Each flash illuminated the buoys just long enough for me to gain a bearing. With lightning-lit buoys guiding the way, I navigated the entrance and slipped into Onset Bay.

Within minutes I found an unoccupied mooring at the Point Independence Yacht Club and tied up for the night. The storms continued to rage on either side but my old boat and her old man continued to enjoy peace and calm in 'The Bubble." If there is a sailor's God out there somewhere he or she was on duty that evening. 1:15am and all was well.

Figure 5-4: Lightning hit near the Buzzard's Bay Railroad Bridge less than a mile away

The following morning dawned clean and fresh but with a fairly strong Northeast wind. If this wind held, it would make for difficult i.e. rough conditions at the Eastern end of the Canal and in Cape Cod Bay. However, the NOAA forecast on the boat's radio forecast a Southwesterly . . . so no need to worry until we reached the Canal's East End marina.

I ate a quick breakfast (cranberry juice, percolator coffee and raisin bran), paid the attendant for the use of the mooring and set out, under power not sail for the Canal (sailing is not allowed in the CCC).

I had timed my departure to coincide with an Easterly flow and, enjoying a boost from the Canal's current, soon found myself zooming along at the ridiculous ground speed of 10+ knots.

About half way through the cut a woman bicycler on the right bank began waving frantically while trying to keep up. I slowed down to half speed and asked what she wanted.

"Are you **Buckrammer**, the woman yelled.

"Sure am," I replied. "Who are you?"

"I'm the Coggeshall scouting party," she replied. "Everyone is waiting for you at the marina. I'm supposed to race back and tell them you've been sighted . . . but at the rate you're traveling you'll probably beat me there." (Cell phones were not yet ubiquitous).

"OK," I shouted back. "See you there, one way or another."

Ben Brewster, one of the Catboat Association's former Presidents, when asked how to make a catboat sail faster, typically replied, "If you wanted to travel fast, you should have bought a bicycle." The thought struck me that, now that **Buckrammer** zipped along in the ferocious Canal current, we just might prove old Ben wrong.

Buckrammer passed beneath the Sagamore bridge and in short order came up on the harbor of refuge at the Canal's East end. A quick turn of the wheel brought the old boat into the sheltered waters of the little marina there.

As predicted, the Coggelshall welcoming party stood at the ready on the quay.

Tim Coggeshall let loose a huge wave. "Ahoy John and ahoy **Buckrammer**. Boy are we glad to see you. We'll hop aboard and navigate you down to Barnstable. Let's go!"

I tossed the dock lines to the assembled crew and made fast to the pilings.

"How are the sea conditions outside?" I asked. "It felt like we had quite Northeast breeze as I came through the Canal."

"Nothing that the old Pelican can't handle, Tim boasted. "Probably a six foot sea or so."

"A six foot sea," I gulped. "Not sure we want to challenge that. Mind if I take a quick walk and check things out?"

Tim nodded. "OK with us. We'll just wait in the boat for you to return."

I climbed up onto the dock and headed toward the beach near the Canal's East entrance. On the way I passed the Harbormaster's shack.

"OK if I leave my old catboat at the dock for a few minutes?"

"You've got 30 minutes before I kick you off," he smiled. But you might want to reserve a slip for the night, due to the sea conditions and all."

"Sea conditions?," I queried.

"Yes, sir," he shot back. With the Canal current and the Nor'East wind fight'n one another we've got a 12 foot breaking sea running at the entrance to the Canal. Once out of the flow you'll face six to eight breakers in Cape Cod Bay. Where'd you say you were heading? P-Town?"

"Nope," I answered. "Barnstable harbor"

"Sorry Cap but no you ain't. Small craft warnings are posted and I'd strongly advise against bringing your catboat into that mess. Soooo . . . Want to rent a slip? Fifty bucks even will do it."

Fifty dollars lighter, I trudged back to the dock to break the news.

Tim resisted but I finally prevailed. "One of the reasons our old boat has lasted so long is that she's had a pampered existence in her dotage. No sense changing that now."

The Coggeshall clan agreed.

"Tell you what," Luby, Tim's wife piped in. "Why don' t we all head back to our family compound, have a cool glass of lemonade and see if the wind dies down?"

Sounded like a great plan to all present. The entourage packed into the two cars and soon found itself in the back yard of the main house in the Coggeshall's Barnstable compound sipping on a frosty glass.

Over the next few hours Tim, Luby and Clark Coggeshall gave me a tour of their little corner of paradise. One of the highlights was a flip through the family photo album packed full of images of **Buckrammer**/Pelican throughout the summers from 1938 to 1954.

"As you can see," Tim explained, "Pelican was an integral part of our family in those summer days. We were heartbroken when it came time to sell her and I suspect that you will suffer the same emotional distress when that time comes for you"

How could I not agree.

"Hey everybody, the wind's died down." One of the many Coggeshall nephews burst into the room. "I think you guys may be able to sail here yet today."

As quick as a cat, the crew remounted the automobiles and headed back to the East End marina.

The Canal tide had turned and now flowed in harmony with the wind, which had dropped from a howling 35 knots to a more respectable 10 to 15.

"And the seas look pretty calm as well . . . about a foot or two.," Clark reported.

"What are we waiting for?" Tim bellowed. "Let's go."

I checked in with the Harbormaster to report that we would not need the slip for the night as planned (no refund, natch), loaded up those crazy enough to join in the sail and shoved off.

Within minutes, **Buckrammer** and company snored along on a due-East heading for Barnstable Harbor, on a Nor'East beam reach with a bone in her teeth. Fantastic.

Each of the boarding party, in turn, took a trick at the wheel. Just outside of Barnstable Harbor we were met head on by another catboat, a Marshall 18 footer. She glided past then tacked around to show us her stern. There, big as life, we could read her name; PELICAN.

"Greetings old Pelican from new Pelican," "I've been wanting to do this for a very long time. Follow me in.". The new Pelican was skippered by Tim's nephew Chad who, I later learned, had grown up on a continuous diet of "old Pelican" sea stories. When it came time to buy a boat of his own, only a catboat would do.

We spent the next hour or so sailing on approach to Barnstable Harbor, old Pelican and new Pelican wing 'n wing. It was a magical experience for all.

Figure 5-5: Captain Conway and the Coggeshall clan head to Barnstable Harbor

Barnstable Harbor is a well-protected, expansive but shallow body of water. The entrance channel runs North-South but the current lies East-West. This, coupled with the ever-shifting sand and mud flats, make for a challenging approach.

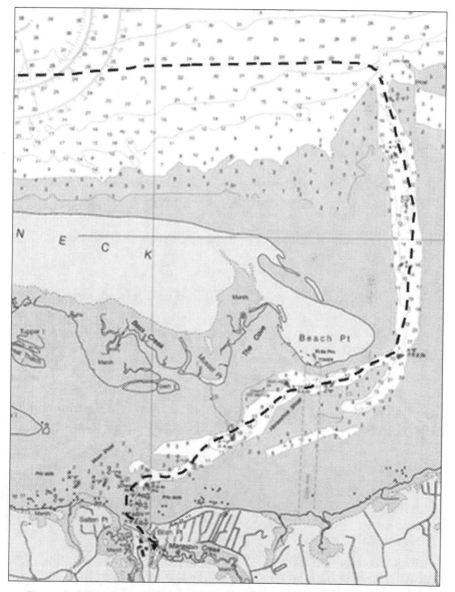

Figure 5-6: We motored **Buckrammer** through the sandbars of Barnstable Harbor

Ever an old salt, Tim urged us to enter under sail. "You can bring her right up to the mooring with her rag up," he suggested. But the rest of the crew, recommended otherwise. So, with a great huff from Tim, we fired up the "cast iron breeze" and opted to motor in.

With Clark at the helm, and lots of helping hands, I began the process of furling the sail. The process began with tightening the topping lift to preven the boom from falling into the cockpit.

TWANG! CRASH! The topping lift parted with a loud report and the main boom came crashing down into the cockpit.

"Good Gawd," I yelled. "Is everyone OK?"

One by one, from under the acres of sail cloth draping the cockpit, each of **Buckrammer**'s guests, in turn, reported in. All OK.

"Whew!" Boy, did I breathe a sigh of relief.

Inspection of the situation revealed that the topping lift line had parted near the top or truck of the mast. An old wooden barrel, mounted on top of the boat's cabin roof, had broken the fall of the 32-foot main boom and sail and had prevented (by an inch or so) anyone from being brained. Too close for comfort.

The experienced hands aboard quickly flakes and gasketed the sail. With the sail all neatly triced, we could use the peak halyard as a pseudo-topping lift to pull the boom-sail combo into their boom crutch.

"Never a dull moment with these old boats, eh?!" Tim commented

With that, everyone broke out into laughter and this quickly deflated the angst aboard.

We motored over to the main dock of the Barnstable Yacht Club and made fast. After a more than 50 year absence, Pelican had returned home.

The rest of the weekend went more or less as planned. That first, Saturday evening, the Club celebrated the 100th anniversary of its founding and both **Buckrammer** and her captain were feted in grand style. After a cake cutting ceremony, we exchanged Catboat Association and BYC burgees and I donated a copy of my previous book, **Catboat Summers,** to the club's library.

During the event we held an open house on the boat and many of the older members came by to share their Pelican experiences, of which there were many . . . some a bit too risqué to repeat here. Net:Net—Pelican was, indeed, the Queen of the Fleet at the BYC in those bygone days.

On Sunday, the Club organized a Parade of Sail with **Buckrammer** in the lead. Several of the members had spent considerable time Sunday morning helping to re-rig a new topping lift so that we could participate under full sail. The new topping lift worked well and the full rag flew.

Figure 5-7: Pelican (aka **Buckrammer**) once again reigns as Queen of the Fleet

After the event, the Coggeshall family once again joined me in Pelican's cockpit.

A bit misty, Tim took firm grasp of my hand, looked me straight in the eyes and gave a squeeze. I think he found my eyes a bit misty as well.

CHAPTER 6

SWALLOWED BY THE WRECK OF THE ANGELA

"I'd like to invite myself to to Edgartown too, but only if I can bring the food and drink." Carol Williamson, a long time Westport friend and master, amateur, Southern-School-of-Cooking chef looked me straight in the eyes in a most serious manner.

"Hmmmm," I salivated, "SURE!"

Thus began what would turn out as one of the more curious, maybe even bizarre of our many **Buckrammer** adventures . . . er, *misadventures*.

Carol, a landscape architect by vocation but an excellent catboat sailor and cook by avocation could be counted on for at least one or two overnight excursions per season with me aboard my old Crosby catboat, **Buckrammer**. We had earlier discussed a number of possibilities for this summer's outing when fate stepped in.

Jim and Kim O'Conner, owners Chef Works, one of Martha's Vineyard's most popular catering services and Jay and Dianne Webster, authors of the "Cat Food" column (i.e cooking aboard catboats) in the Catboat Association's quarterly magazine, had just completed the first leg of their annual joint cruise along the south Massachusetts coast and found themselves in my homeport of Westport, Massachusetts.

"We're heading back to MV this weekend," Jim teased. "Why not join us? We're shooting for Edgartown and should arrive just in time for the CBA Rendezvous. Come on!"

Jim explained that he, Kim and the Websters planned to reach Edgartown in two legs.

They would overnight in Cuttyhunk as the first leg from Westport and the following day would make the long sail to Edgartown as the second leg. If all went according to plan, they would arrive in Edgartown just in time for the annual, epic, Edgartown catboat race sponsored by the Catboat Association.

Jay joined in. "Come on John. The forecast is perfect, the seas calm and the boats ready. We can convoy and keep each other out of trouble should any arise. This will be cake."

"Cake!"

"OK! I'm in," I agreed.

Carol provisioned **Buckrammer** as only he could with a wide assortment of exotic foodstuffs and potables. From the looks of it we would be eating (and drinking?) most of our way to Edgartown in a style significantly beyond **Buckrammer**'s typical, pedestrian manner.

Later that afternoon the catboats **Glimmer** (O'Connor's), **Ishmael** (Webster's) and **Buckrammer** set our sights for Cuttyhunk, about 10 miles away, and headed out.

After an uneventful, pleasant sail, our "convoy" arrived at the little island just in time for the cocktail hour, about 5:00pm. (**Figure 6-1**)

Rather than moor in the crowded Cuttyhunk Inner Harbor, we decided to anchor as a raft-up (i.e tied together) in the Outer Harbor near the entrance to the Canapitsit Channel, a local-knowledge shortcut into Vineyard Sound. This anchorage would position us to get a jump on our departure when the tide turned early next morning. Experience had long ago shown that sailboats could enjoy a two to three-knot boost by riding the current in the Sound . . . and we planned to ride it all the way to Edgartown.

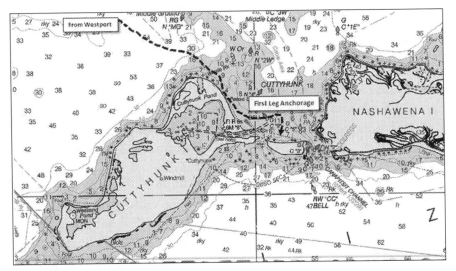

Figure 6-1: The route from Westport to Cuttyhunk to our anchorage area.

"Here! Try one of these oysters. They're a new variety from Nantucket" Jim handed Carol and me a few succulent bivalves along with a small bowl of spicy cocktail sauce and some lemon slices.

After a quick slurp, Carol dashed below, retrieved a slab of his famous smoked Bluefish pate, some triple-cream brie, pepper jelly and a basket of rye toasts and began distributing them around.

"This pate is one of my specialties," Carol boasted. "Combine the pate with a smidge of brie and jelly on the rye crisps and go to heaven."

We did as instructed and entered through Carol's Pearly Gates.

Needless to say, the next few hours were spent with each of these food masters trying to outdo one another with all manner of wonderful eatables. I manned the bar and discovered the most popular potable to be the Dark & Stormy . . . A blend of strong Gosling's Black Seal rum, ginger beer (NOT ginger ale), a good squeeze of and a slice of lime all over ice.

Heaven indeed.

(Side Note: It was especially poetic that Gosling's was our rum of choice. Bartholomew *Gosnold* "discovered" Cuttyhunk Island in 1602 during an expedition to what would ultimately become New England. A monument to him stands in the middle of the island. Since Goslings and Gosnold are almost one and the same and to honor the spirit of this great adventurer, who, among other accomplishments gave Cape Cod and Martha's Vineyard their names, we were forced to consume several more Dark and Stormy's than normal. Seemed only right and proper.)

We all slept MOST soundly that first night.

The following morning came all too quickly and would have been a perfect specimen of an early summer sailing day with one exception, *no wind*.

Scanning the scene, Jay piped up, "Maybe the wind will pick up after breakfast and if not, we'll just motor until it does."

Seemed like a plan

The O'Connors served Eggs Benedict for all (not sure how they accomplished this on a catboat stove) and I made several pots of strong coffee in **Buckrammer**'s old percolator.

We all enjoyed this wonderful breakfast while wishing for a wind to rise but come the turn of the tide Mother Nature had yet to conjure up even a wisp.

Jim consulted his watch. "Time to shove off if we are to catch the Vineyard Sound sleigh ride. Let's uncouple, hoist anchors and shoot the channel."

In rapid succession we did just that, fired up our auxiliaries and moved into the Canapitsit passage. (**Figure 6-2**)

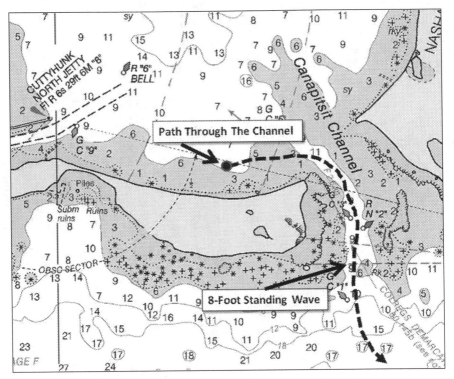

Figure 6-2: The route through the Canapitsit Channel

Most of the cruising guides to this area strongly advise against boaters accessing Vineyard Sound through the Canapitsit Channel unless you are really familiar with the passage. Several reasons for this are mentioned:

1. There can be a very strong current, as much as a 2.6 knots, running in the channel because a good portion of Buzzard's Bay is often trying to pass through this little knot hole of an opening. The current has been known to cause mariner's to lose steering control and spin their boats around.

2. As shown in **Figure 6-2**, large, sharp rocks line either side of the channel. An out-of-control boat could quickly find its bottom torn away.

3. As the tide empties through the sluice from Buzzard's Bay it encounters the incoming current from Vineyard Sound. This creates a standing train of waves that can reach ten feet or more . . . *on a good day.* And 20 feet or

more on a bad one . . . waves that can easily broach and swamp a small craft of 65 feet or less.

So it was with more than a little trepidation that I decided to bring **Buckrammer** into Vineyard Sound this way. However, both Jim and Jay had done this many, many times and they would lead the way. So I thought, "What the Hell?"

Glimmer entered first with Ishmael close behind. I decided to hold back a bit to see how these lead boats fared. Within seconds it became obvious that the standing wave had both boats in its grip as they bounced up and down, in and out of view as the almost three knot current swept them though the sluice.

Carol gave me a concerned glare. "Looks like there's a four or six foot wave train in the channel. Think we should do this?"

I was tempted to say "No" but **Buckrammer** was already committed to the run as the current had us in its grip as well.

"Hold onto your knickers," I yelled to Carol. "It's gonna be a wild ride."

And wild ride it was. Imagine five and a half tons of wooden boat being tossed up and down like a plaything and you'll have some sense of the experience. Unsecured pots, pans and other loose stuff below went flying. **Buckrammer**'s main boom swung wildly back and forth and our old Girl rocked violently from side to side.

In an earlier life I had done consulting work for the Professional Bullriders Association. While I never actually rode a bull I witnessed many a young cowboy do so . . . and now, aboard our bucking catboat, I felt a kinship with those brave souls.

"YeeHaw!"

My greatest fear was that we might spring a plank or stall the engine but, somehow, everything held together and kept running. In less than five minutes of terror we punched through into the glass-calm (i.e. no wind) waters of Vineyard Sound.

Carol looked at me and gave a hearty laugh. "How about that, we're still alive!"

Up ahead, Jim, Jay and company throttled up and pulled ahead.

Carol volunteered to take a trick at **Buckrammer**'s helm.

"Better throttle up as well," I barked to Carol, "Jim and Jay are leaving us in the dust."

"Aye, aye skipper," Carol obeyed and gave Red, Jr., our trusty diesel a bit more fuel.

Almost immediately the engine began to sputter and we quickly lost about half of our forward speed. To my ear it sounded like one or two (of the four) fuel injectors were not firing. Carol noticed the problem as well.

I instructed Carol to keep us on course while I tried to nurse the still running but clearly ill engine back to life.

I pulled off the engine cover and grabbed a 5/8 open end injector wrench. My initial thought was that the rough ride through Canapitsit had put a few air bubbles in the fuel lines and that one or more of these had air-bound some of the injectors. If so, this would be an easy fix as all I had to do was bleed the air out of the injector by loosening the injector nut, wait for fuel to flow, then retighten everything.

I proceeded with the operation and the engine roared back to her normal self . . . until I replaced the engine cover that is. In less than a minute the problem reoccurred

"Damn," I remember thinking. Repeated attempts to bleed the system proved fruitless and after the fifth attempt the engine just conked out.

I now suspected that the bouncy ride through the Canapitsit has shaken loose some crud from the bottom of our fuel tank and that this had somehow wormed its way into the injectors and clogged them up. (We later learned that this was caused by B100 biodiesel mixing with normal diesel and it all turning into diesel pudding, See **Chapter 2**)

"Not a problem," I explained to my frustrated helmsman. "We have the outboard as back-up and that will see us through. We can worry about the diesel when we moor in Edgartown this afternoon."

For many years we had hung a 4HP gas outboard off of **Buckrammer**'s stern. We were always amazed that such a little motor could push around such a large and heavy boat as **Buckrammer** . . . but it could. Not only did we use it for emergency back-up and thin water propulsion (to avoid sucking mud into the diesel's cooling system) but we also found a use for the little thing as a maneuvering thruster for navigating in tight spaces and gunkholes.

A few pulls on the starter cord fired the outboard to life and our catboat was once again underway.

In the interim, Glimmer and Ishmael had pulled a considerable distance away from us. I went below and tried to hail them on our radio. No luck! After numerous attempts on channels 16, 9 and 72 (universal hailing, local hailing and catboat hailing frequencies respectively) I gave up. (I later learned that neither Glimmer nor Ishmael had their radios turned on and would not do so until they reached Edgartown. Make a note . . . When boating, *remember to leave your radio on!*)

"No matter," I boasted to Carol. "We'll catch up with them when we reach Edgartown."

Carol smiled and nodded in agreement just as the outboard coughed, backfired, wheezed and stopped.

"You've got to be kidding me," I muttered as repeated attempts to restart the motor also failed.

"Arrrgggghhhh"

Carol, still at the wheel, squinted at me.

"Well John, we are a sailboat. Maybe we should try raising the sail and see if we can regain motion that way?"

While the wind remained mostly absent, it seemed worth a try.

I unlashed the sail ties, loosened the mainsheet, unseated the main boom from its crutch hauled on the halyards and unfurled the magnificent gaff sail that gave **Buckrammer** her wing. Nothing! The Sound remained a sheet of windless glass. The reefing points on the sail just tapped their little tappity-tap sound signaling "the sail ain't work'n."

"Arrrrrrggggggghhhhhh!"

"This is turning out to be an interesting cruise," Carol smiled. "Indeed another **Buckrammer** adventure, *I love it.*"

All I could do was laugh. An adventure indeed.

OK . . . So what to do? The Vineyard Sound current moved us north and east at about two knots. At this rate, assuming no wind, (in about 6 hours) we would make land somewhere around West Chop, a nasty spot appropriately named for the confused sea conditions found there. Not really an acceptable option.

"Let me try the engines once again" I said to Carol. "You never know"

"Worth a shot," he replied.

I cranked over the diesel until her starter motor began smoking. Nothing.

I next gave a few tugs on the outboard and, IT STARTED!!! And, more importantly, kept running.

"Eureka!"

We were once again underway.

This lasted all of 10 minutes when the motor once again stalled and stopped.

This placed us just off of the north western shore of Nashawena Island near the Quick's Hole passage between Buzzard's Bay and the Sound. (**Figure 6-3**)

"I hate to do this to you Carol, but I feel that we should abandon our Edgartown expedition attempt and try to return to Westport. The Gods are clearly against us right now."

Carol, good natured soul that he is, agreed.

"I can't imagine navigating through the West and East Chops without some form of reliable propulsion," he commented. "Back to Westport it is."

Just then a half knot tease of wind arose . . . enough for us to regain steering but barely enough to move us more than a half of a mile an hour.

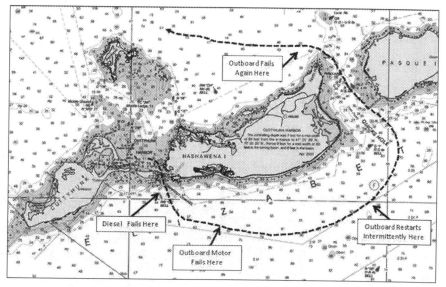

Figure 6-3: The drift path around Nashawena Island

Slowly our 5.5 ton woodpile turned into Quick's Hole where we picked up a little boost from the 1 knot of current running into the Bay.

After a few minutes, I tried to restart the outboard once more and once again it worked.

"Gaaaa!"

The little engine that could slowly propelled us into the hole for another ten minutes or so before once again giving up the ghost.

"I think I know what's up with the motor," I commented to Carol. Something like this happened to me and my brother long ago when my folks had a summer cottage on Onset Island further up in Buzzard's Bay."

Intrigued, Carol asked, "OK doctor, what is your prognosis and can we fix it?"

"I think it's the unit's temperature sensor. The temperature sensor is designed to detect a problem due to overheating . . . . as in, if the motor overheats the sensors tell it to shut down before any damage occurs. If the sensor fails it shuts things down at the wrong temp. I bet that's what's happening.

Carol inquired "Can you fix it?"

"Sadly, no," I answered. "But it does mean that we can run the outboard in 10 minute bursts with, say, 10 to 15 minute rests in between to cool down. Not the best way to motor home but limping our way back is way better than not getting back at all.

BEEP-BEEP-BEEP-BEEP

The shallow water alarm on the boat's depth sounder came alive.

While not paying attention, the current had set **Buckrammer** over the rocky reef that forms the southern end of Pasque Island, on the northern side of Quick's.

Our only hope of avoiding disaster was to motor our way out of this trap.

"Please start, please start, please start," I remember praying to the outboard.

She had only been cooling for a few minutes so I had my doubts.

Several tugs on the starter cords proved ineffective. However, miraculously, on the third try she sputtered to life.

"There is a God" I exclaimed as **Buckrammer** slowly made her way back into the center of the channel and far away from danger.

Carol just nodded and smiled his wry smile, "As I said John, an interesting cruise."

Over the next few hours the **Buckrammer** and her two ancient mariners crept our way past Penekese Island and across the lower end of Buzzard's Bay in ten minutes ON, ten minutes OFF motor bursts. The wind remained absent, an exceptionally unusual condition for an area world famous for its dependably strong winds. We did eat well however.

"I've got food for a week down below," Carole reminded us. "Might as well break out a feast, eh?!"

And we did just that. Never before or since have I consumed as many calories while crossing Buzzard's Bay.

A little before 1:00pm we found ourselves just south of the treacherous Hens and Chickens reef near the approach to Westport off of Gooseberry Point. Over the centuries, the "Hen's" had claimed over 1200 ships in transit along the South Coast of Massachusetts. In fact, the Massachusetts Humane Society, one of the precursors to the U.S. Coast Guard, in 1888 had built one of its few life saving stations on the beach near the reef order to rescue those in distress. (**Figure 6-4**)

(From 2007 to 2009 the Westport Fisherman's association raised funds and restored this amazing historical station. It now operates as a living museum.)

We planned to motor around this hazardous area but once again, the Sea Gods had other ideas.

Figure 6-4: The restored Westport Life Saving station near Hens & Chicken's

As shown in **Figure 6-5,** the southern end of the reef is known as The Wildcat. On the western edge of this boulder field lies the wreck of the motorized cement barge, **Angela.**

As reported on the home page of MishaumPoint.com., *"The Angela was designed and built in 1962-63 for the specific job of transporting dry cement. She and her two sisters were the largest ocean going cement barges in the world. She was 425 feet long and 8512 gross tons. Her design was considered unique in that she was unmanned and self loading. Her two enormous screw augers extended three-quarters the length of the barge. There function was to mix the dry cement with air, and move it forward to be placed into silos on shore. In April 1971 the Angela was in tow with over 70,000 barrels of cement heading for Boston via the Cape Cod Canal. With very dense fog and a building sea, the tow hawser parted. The captain of the tug decided to anchor his tow (he was able to do this using a remote control device). He then placed two crew on the barge to check the anchor and finding it secure, sought shelter in New Bedford to wait out the fog and seas. The changing current meanwhile swung the heavy barge onto the nearby Hens and Chicken Reef. When the captain returned he found his barge squarely impaled on top of Old Cock rock. When divers were finally able to check her hull, they found extensive damage. Some salvage was conducted, her two diesel engines that operated the screw augers were recovered, and her diesel fuel was removed."*

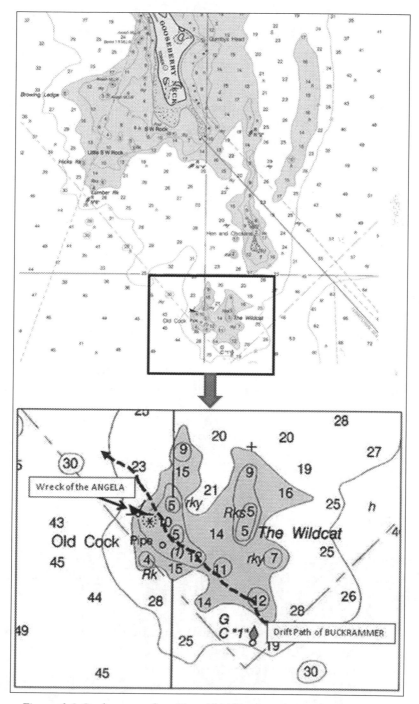

Figure 6-5: Buckrammer found herself drifting into the treacherous Wildcat

The wreck sits slightly visible atop the Wildcat to this day. While it provides a home for numerous sport fish and an easy wreck for divers to explore, the Angela and her surroundings serve as a No Man's Land for boats of almost any size.

The hidden rocks coupled with unpredictable whirkpools and surges loudly broadcast KEEP AWAY. And Carol and I clearly intended to do just that, except . . .

The outboard motor died once and for all just as we approached this notorious piece of ocean. Without thrust, the prevailing current would set **Buckrammer** on a collision course with every hazard that the Wildcat offered.

"This could be REALLY interesting, John," Carol, a bit wide-eyed, commented.

I quickly agreed, thinking something like "We'll all gonna die."

The one thing working in our favor was the calm sea conditions. There was a slight surge or swell running but no breakers. So the Wildcat was not as wild as we had seen her on past voyages.

None the less, our drift clearly moved us through the Wildcat's underwater rock garden, past the massive Old Cock boulder and closer and closer to the massive shipwreck.

BUMP-BUMP-BUMP-BUMP

Buckrammer's centerboard came in contact with several underwater obstructions and swung up (a marvelous feature of centerboards as opposed to fixed keels)

I quickly ran to the centerboard winch and cranked the board fully up. In the down position the board drew 6 feet or more. When up, the entire catboat only needed two feet of water to run safely.

"Look just below the surface to starboard," Carol commanded. "That is one, mother, boat crunching rock." In the clear, calm water less than two feet from her hull about one foot under water, **Buckrammer** glided past a massive stone.

I felt some of Carol's wonderful comestibles moving their way back up my throat.

"Scheeesssh! That was close," I wimpered.

The photos **of Figure 6-6** shows the sequence of events.

Tide, storms and time had, over the years, broken the back of the massive, old barge. As a result she now lay in two pieces with a collapsed, debris and knife-like, steel plate-strewn booby trap in what was once her center section (**Figure 6-6a**).

As the wreck loomed ever closer the thought struck me that, much like Jonah, **Buckrammer** was about to be swallowed by the center section of the wrecked Leviathan. We were headed straight for the dead center section and were powerless to do a damn thing about it. Worse, the chart showed that a very large boulder, probably the one that sank the vessel in the first place, lay just in front of the center section gap. So if the wreck didn't snare us the rock certainly would

I tried to start both the diesel and the outboard to no avail. Within minutes we would be trapped within the mid-section of the beast.

I whispered to Carol, "Prayer would be appreciated my friend." He silently nodded.

We drifted closer still. Close enough that we could see the wreckage that would probably slice through our hull. (**Figure 6-6b**)

"When we get close enough to touch metal (or rock) maybe we can fend off?" I asked Carol who instinctively ran forward and retrieved our boat hook.

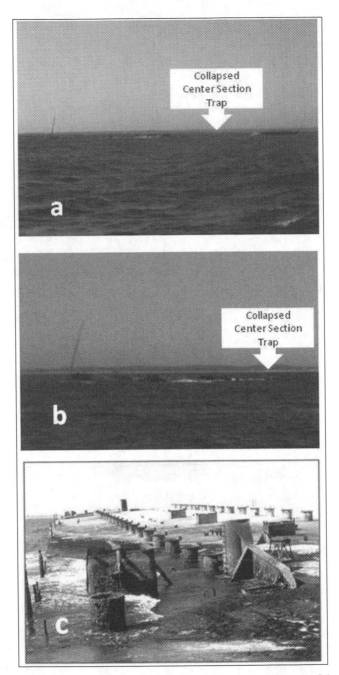

Figure 6-6: Buckrammer headed straight for the collapsed center section of the wreck and came close enough for her crew to spit upon the massive thing.
(Photo 6C by David Clancy from WreckHunter.net)

"No harm in trying,"

As Carol moved to position himself along the port quarter to try to push us away from the wreck, a miracle occurred.

The wind came up and the sail filled.

"Holy shitake mushrooms (or something similar)," I yelled. "We're sailing."

Quickly Carol jumped back into the cockpit and took the wheel while I adjusted the mainsheet and halyards.

Buckrammer slowly veered to starboard just skirting the starboard side of the Angela. We were within ten feet of the rusted steel hull, but did not collide; close enough to spit at the wretched thing, which we did. (**Figure 6-6c**).

Once out of harm's way Carol and I brought **Buckrammer** into the wind, luffed up and danced a very happy jig in the old bucket's cockpit.

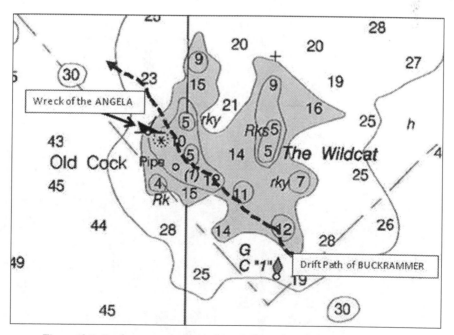

Figure 6-7: **Buckrammer** had somehow drift navigated through the Wildcat

My son, Ned, had given me a bottle of Ardbeg Uigeadail single malt scotch (distilled pine tar as far as I'm concerned) that we kept below for special occasions.

Ile of Islay whiskey never tasted as sweet.

CHAPTER 7

WATSONS' ANNIVERSARY SURPRISE

"Hello! My name is Jacob Watson. Our family used to own your catboat and I've got a very big favor to ask."

Chris and I had just arrived in Westport for an early Spring weekend (aka house cleaning)

As I unloaded the car, Chris scrolled through the voice mail messages accumulated by our answering machine during the previous weeks. Jacob Watson's was among them.

"Hey John!,' she yelled from the front porch. "Do you know anyone named Watson? He says that his family owned our boat."

It took a few seconds for me to process . . . "Watson, hmmmm, Watson . . . ."

The it hit me like the proverbial tone of bricks.

"OMYGAWD!," I yelled back, "I think this must be the Saltonstall/Watsons. If so, they were the owners of **Buckrammer** during the Great Depression," I gasped. "Did they leave a number? Yes? Then quick . . . give me the phone."

Thus began one of the most heartwarming of our many **Buckrammer** adventures.

The phone number had a Down East Maine area code. As I dialed I wondered what in the world Jacob ever have in mind.

After a few rings, the receiver picked up. "Hello, this is Reverend Watson."

In short order I learned that Jacob was the son of Hoyt and Anne Watson.

"I read your book Catboat Summers, Jacob explained," and was delighted to see that the catboat owned by my father still actively sailed. We thought that she had been lost in Hurricane Carol in the early 1950's." "As you know, when he had the boat she operated as the Josephine S. You probably do not know that she was rechristened in 1932 to honor my father's newborn niece, Josephine Saltonstall." Jacob continued. "Dad moored the boat in front of the family summer home on Allen's Point in Marion, Massachusetts, enjoyed her for a number of years and had numerous adventures in the thing along the New England coast. I'd love to think that he and mum could have one more Josephine S experience."

Jacob continued, "This August mum and dad will celebrate their 65th wedding anniversary and the family intends to hold a gala anniversary event. Is there any chance that we could rent your boat for that event weekend? It played a major role in my dad's life and in mum and dad's courtship."

I quickly replied, "I wouldn't be interested in renting **Buckrammer** but rather, I'd be delighted to sail her back to Marion and host the extended Watson/Saltonstall family for a weekend of as much catboating as they could stomach."

Jacob quickly accepted the offer.

"Let's keep in touch over the coming months," I suggested. "As we get closer to the date we can finalize plans." Jacob agreed and, as the saying goes, the game was afoot.

The anniversary weekend came on us with amazing rapidity.

Figure 7.1-The author, Buckrammer and Splinter (dinghy) prepare to head out
(Photo Courtesy of Jim O'Connor)

Jacob and I had evolved a simple plan:

1. **Buckrammer** would depart from Westport on Friday around 8:00am with an estimated time of arrival in Marion harbor of ~2:00pm

2. Around noon, Jacob and his co-conspirators would innocently gather everyone on the lawn facing the harbor for an extended anniversary lunch.

3. Around 2:00 pm I would sail **Buckrammer** up to the Watson/Saltonstall family dock on Allen's Point in the harbor in full view of the lunch party.

4. From there we'd make things up as we went.

Anniversary Friday arrived and I spent the early morning hours tidying up **Buckrammer** and prepping her for the voyage ahead. I assumed that I would be sleeping on the boat over the weekend, so I stored provisions and all of the gear and claptrap necessary. Competing activities prevented my wife, Chris, and all of the Conway kids from joining in on the fun. So this would be a solo adventure.

With clear skies and a freshening southwester, the old bucket and her graying captain slipped from the mooring under auxiliary power and headed out.

Like most catboats her size, **Buckrammer** is a lot of vessel to single hand under sail. Nevertheless, if one follows a step-by-step process with an attitude of safety-first and an "if anything can go wrong it will . . . and at the worst possible time" frame of mind, then the experience can be quite rewarding.

For our old Crosby cat, this means:

1. Always wear a lifejacket when "flying solo." (For man overboard accidents)

2. Trail about 50+ feet of line with a torpedo buoy on the bitter end off the transom.
    (Also for overboard situations . . . to pull yourself back to the boat before she sails away)

3. Hoist and unfurl (or lower and furl) the boat's sail in calm, wide open water if possible (i.e. not a crowded mooring area or main channel).

4. Follow a structured procedure for #3. To wit:

    a. Engine running, point the boat into the wind
        (Nice to have the engine at-the-ready in case it's needed)
    b. Set the topping lift line tight
    c. Remove all of the sail ties
    d. Remove the "horse rope"
    e. line that secures the boom in the boom crutch)
    f. Loosen the main sheet a tad (but take a turn on the main sheet cleat)

g. Lift the boom out of the crutch with the topping lift line and re-cleat the line g. Remove the boom crutch and stow (typically on a cockpit seat)

h. Loosen the throat and peak halyards

i. Hoist the sail (taking care that the gaff boom lies to port of the toping lift)

j. Secure the throat halyard

k. Continue to hoist the peak halyard until a wrinkle appears near the sail luff

l. Loosen the topping lift and re-cleat

m. Take the helm and bear off while setting the main sheet to a proper scope

n. Kill the engine

Executed properly and with enough experience, #4 takes all of about two minutes to complete. It's an almost "autopilot" kind of task.

All of this in mind, I motored down the Westport River to an area ideal for executing #4. In no time at all, **Buckrammer**'s sail filled, we exited the harbor and set a northerly course in a long, graceful arc that would curve us from Rhode Island Sound into and along the Western shore of Buzzard's Bay.

With winds blowing around 12 knots and seas running with a chop of about two feet, the boat cruised at hull speed . . . about 6.5 knots . . . and quickly passed the familiar landmarks of Gooseberry Island, the Slocum River, Mishaum Point and Padanaram.

"At this rate of speed," I remember thinking, "I'll be in Marion well before 2 o'clock."

As the boat transited the historic whaling port of New Bedford, we passed through (actually probably barged through) two sailboat races hosted by the New Bedford Yacht Club. Formed in 1877, the NBYC is one of the oldest in America.

Etchells 30-footers, about a dozen boats in all, comprised one of the race fleets. The other appeared to be Rhodes 19's. Both the Etchells and Rhodes boats zoomed along towards their respective marks, at a rate of speed considerably faster than my old girl. The crews on these boats exchanged glances with me as I bee-lined through their race courses and tried my best not to disrupt their respective quests. I figured that it wasn't every day that these plastic boat sailors encountered a 100 year-old vessel mid-race.

Figure 7.2: Buckrammer almost barges through an NBYC Etchells-30 race

Having buzzed the fleets, **Buckrammer** continued her curvaceous course north and soon left West Island, a spit of land just east and north of New Bedford, behind.

The typically strong, south/southwest wind (half jokingly referred to as the afternoon Buzzard's Bay Hurricane) had been mostly on our beam up until now. But as our course bent more north than east the wind landed more on our stern and our broad reach became more of a fast run.

In addition, the tide had also turned from flood to ebb. The outgoing tide and incoming wind created an ever building swell and soon we ourselves in fairly dramatic, six foot following seas.

I had our dinghy, Splinter (See **Catboat Summers**), under tow. In normal conditions, the little rowboat just tugs along behind the mothership. However, a following sea changes the dynamic entirely. On the front side of a swell, the dinghy can race down the face of the wave with such speed and force that it sometimes leaps right out of the water and into the cockpit of the tow-boat. Not good. On the back side of a swell, the dinghy can submarine as its tow-line (i.e. painter) tries to pull it through the rising wall of water.

To reduce the risks of either scenario, you can either pull the dinghy aboard the mothership (not really an option for **Buckrammer**) or shorten the tow-line such that the smaller boat nestles right up against the stern of the bigger boat. This is the course of action I decided to take.

The trick to doing this successfully is all in the timing.

Ideally all I had to do was wait for the dinghy to begin its race down the swell and just (just!) quickly pull in the painter, hand-over-hand, to keep the little boat under control. When I had the boat close to the stern, I would quickly cleat-off the tow-line (aka painter) and voila!, the dinghy woulds now be in a safe place (more or less).

This exercise would prove a bit more challenging today because I had no one to help me . . . but not outrageously challenging . . . or at least I thought.

Waves travel in measured cycles and I watched and mentally timed the frequency and period of those playing with Splinter. Just as I was about to grab the painter and do my thing, an out-of-sequence rogue wave arose and the little boat disappeared from view behind it. As I watched in disbelief, Splinter's painter stretched to the breaking point and "twang", snapped like an old rubber band; 3/8th nylon parted as if it were a piece of knitting yarn.

"Oh Gawd! She's submerged," I groaned . . . for Splinter was nowhere to be seen.

Suddenly, the dinghy popped up about 25 feet behind **Buckrammer**, swamped but still afloat.

"Whoa!"

As I doddled, my old catboat continued to sail full speed ahead and poor Splinter drifted ever further behind.

What to do?

The rational, safety-first (my safety, that is) part of me advised . . . "Just let her go. You could put *everything* at risk trying to recapture Splinter in these wind and water conditions." The reckless side of me screamed "You can't let Splinter slip away. You and the kids built her from scratch. She's been a part of the family for over 20 years. You MUST try to salvage her. You MUST. (and, by the way, she would become a hazard to navigation for others in this condition)"

Long story short, recklessness won out that day (mostly) and the rescue attempt commenced.

Challenge that it would be to recover Splinter, it would be even more so under full sail in freshening winds and rough seas, I figured. So I brought **Buckrammer** into the wind, luffed up and furled and secured all ~750 square feet or so of her sail. I then fired up the diesel, came about and headed back towards the dinghy . . . now barely visible about an eighth of a mile astern.

As **Buckrammer** came up on the little boat it gave me a chance to evaluate her condition. Though half full of seawater, her gunwales rode above sea-level. This meant that I'd be able to pump her out once recaptured. The trick now was how to do so.

I passed Splinter to port, then swung around and came broadside with a boat-width between us. The seas were now about 4 to 5 feet with breakers from time to time and the winds blew around 15 to 20 knots. I feared that a wave might just pick up the dinghy and smash it into **Buckrammer**'s side.

As my old catboat and Splinter kept station with one another I noticed that about 10 feet of line remained attached to the eyebolt on Splinter's prow. With a bit of luck, I reasoned, I might be able to snag that line with my boathook and use it to secure Splinter to one of **Buckrammer**'s stern cleats.

"What the Hell," I thought, "Worth a shot."

Long story short, it took three extremely frustrating and very wet attempts to hook the line and cleat it off, but somehow I managed to pull it off without injury to boats or self.

With Splinter now secured close to the **Buckrammer**'s transom, I once again pointed into the wind and heaved to. To get the water out I tied a bailing bucket to a stout line, threw the bucket into the dinghy and, bucket by bucket, hauled most of the brine out of the boat.

The entire operation took about 20 minutes but seemed like an hour . . . . No . . . more like a day. Anyway the catboat, the dinghy and the captain were all finally, safely back together and the journey to Marion Harbor continued.

I decided to motor the remainder of the way and, with the wind at my back, made great if somewhat sloppy progress.

Round about 2:00pm **Buckrammer** passed the Number 3 gong buoy that signals the approach to Sippican (aka Marion) Harbor.

"How 'bout dat," I remember thinking. "Right on time." Now to find the Watson homestead.

Jacob Watson had dictated fairly straightforward instructions, to wit:

"Pass Ram Island to starboard and head for red nun buoy #8. Pass the nun and head for the green # 9 can. Hang a sharp right at the can and set a course for Allen's Point. The "signature" of the Watson dock is a large frame of timbers shaped like the Greek letter Pi Find the Pi-frame and you've found the Watsons."

I followed the Reverend's directions . . . to the letter . . . and headed for the clearly visible structure.

Jacob and the other family members later reported the scene from the Watson compound's perspective.

"As planned, the family had set up an anniversary luncheon on the lawn above the docks." My father was first to spy the old catboat approaching and remarked that it looked much like the one he used to own and sail in his teens and twenties. As the boat grew larger so did father's curiosity." "My Gawd", he remarked, "If I didn't know any better I'd swear that *was* my old Josephine. She looked just like that.

Figure 7.3: Hoyt Watson cannot believe his eyes (with daughter Lea)
(Photo Courtesy of the Watson family)

Dad called the boat to my mother's attention. "Anne . . . Look at that old catboat coming this way. Does that look like the Josephine or not?" "It does," she replied.

As **Buckrammer**/Josephine S continued to head in, Hoyt and Anne began to walk down the hill towards the dock. Soon both **Buckrammer** and the Watsons found themselves racing toward the outer float.

Back aboard I saw a large number of people gathered on the lawn and knew that I had found the old girl's former home. As **Buckrammer** and I closed in on the dock, the crowd began to move down the lawn toward the water. By the time I swung to port and sidled up to the float the entire anniversary party had gathered dockside. Many hands grabbed and secured my dock lines.

Hoyt came right up to the cockpit looking somewhat dumbfounded.

I extended my hand over the coaming and said,

"Mr. Watson, your Josephine S has returned home."

Figure 7.4: Hoyt Watson greets the author and Buckrammer (former Josephine S)
(Photo Courtesy of the Watson family)

Shaking my hand, Hoyt was speechless . . . . but not for long.

"I'll be darned, I'll be darned, I'll be darned," he sputtered. "Permission to come aboard?"

"Granted," I gladly replied.

With a spring in his step, Hoyt clambered aboard and began his inspection. In short order a line of family members cued up, Anne in the lead, all asking if they could explore their beloved Josephine S . . . and explore they did.

The extended boarding party examined, poked, tested, prodded, twisted and thumped virtually every nook and cranny of the old bucket. Comments flowed from Hoyt in rapid succession.

"Hmmm . . . Her wheel is tighter than I remember. What is that outboard doing there? You've converted the water cistern into a rope locker. Ahh . . . The old Shipmate #2 stove is still here. Hmmm. There's a door on the head . . . used to be a curtain. What happened to the bait well? Look . . . She still carries the same documentation numbers". . . and on, and on.

Anne Watson introduced me to Hoyt's family and friends as they boarded. Aunts, uncles, brothers, sisters kids, grandkids and neighbors all had their turn.

One of the more remarkable of these visitors was Katharyn (Kathie) Saltonstall, the wonderfully opinionated spouse of the late Bill (Salty) Saltonstall and Hoyt's sister.

Kathie extended her arms just as she was about to board and, with a twinkle in her 89-year old eyes, exclaimed . . . "I can't wait to see this old thing fly. How soon can we shove off, Cap?"

"First thing tomorrow", I laughed.

(I later learned that, among her many laudable achievements, Kathie was a skilled skipper of Herreshoff 12 footers, raced in Adams Cup sailing championships, and was the author of the popular **Small Bridges to One World**, a memoir of her adventures in the Peace Corps)

However, the most jaw dropping member of the family (as far as my old catboat was concerned) had yet to be introduced.

Figure 7.5: Katherine Saltonstall Moore's heart soars aboard the old catboat
(Photo Courtesy of the Watson family)

"John," Anne Watson offered, "I'd like you to meet Josephine Saltonstall. As you may not know, Joey was born about the same time that Hoyt took ownership of your catboat. He thought it would be good luck to name the vessel Josephine S after his newborn niece."

With that Josephine extended her hand and said "Yep! I'm the namesake of the old girl."

It was my turn to shake hands speechlessly.

We spent the remainder of the afternoon reliving the many adventures that Hoyt and Anne had in the Josephine S. As current caretaker of the old bucket, I relished every tale as each filled in one hole after another in the boat's remarkable past.

For example . . . I learned that Hoyt had been *given* the boat for his 16th birthday (!) and enjoyed many summers cruising her in the waters of Buzzards Bay, the Cape & Islands and, even Down East on occasion. I learned that he would often sail single-handed to Martha's Vineyard and back non-stop; That he almost shipwrecked the boat while passing through Woods Hole in a thunderstorm; and so on.

Figure 7.6: Josephine Saltonstall, revisits her namesake vessel
(Photo Courtesy of the Watson family)

One of his favorite Josephine S adventures involved an extended cruise from Marion, MA north along the New England coast to the New Hampshire/Maine border and up the Piscatqua River with Bill Saltonstall. While passing through one of the Boston & Maine drawbridges in the river, Josephine's mast snagged telegraph lines that had sagged exceptionally low due to the high heat of the summer sun that day. Hoyt did not notice the problem until several hundred feet of wire had been ripped from the signal poles. In trying to extricate the mast and boat, he and Bill snapped the lines and they fell into the river. Somehow the bridge attendant never noticed and Hoyt, crew, boat and all sheepishly crept onward up-river.

On the return trip, however, as they rounded the bend and the bridge hove into view, all aboard spied a railroad work crew re-rigging the lines.

As the boat moved close to the bridge, the foreman signaled Hoyt to heave to. Hoyt was certain that he was about to be arrested . . . *or shot*. After about ten minutes of orbiting on the western side of the bridge The Man motioned that Hoyt could proceed.

As the Josephine S. passed through the raised draw, the attendant yelled from the bridge-house . . . "Sorry about the delay. Some dang vandals cut the lines a day or two ago and we've had a deuce of a time trying to put things back in order."

Hoyt gave a quick salute and motored through.

"I don't think that I took a single breath until we had sailed about a mile or two downstream of that span" he admitted.

We gammed all afternoon and into the early evening.

Hoyt noticed that I had the Splinter on a short leash and I told him of my ordeal.

"Hmmm," he mumbled. We'll have to do something about that."

Anne asked if I would join them for dinner. I explained that I needed to return to Westport to attend a fundraiser for the Watershed Alliance and that my daughter would pick me up.

"We've got a million cars here," Jacob chimed in. "Why not save your daughter a trip and borrow one of ours. You can bring it back tomorrow when we go out to sail."

Seemed like a reasonable and generous offer and I accepted.

Figure 7.7: The Watsons and Saltonstalls gam for hours aboard Buckrammer
(Photo Courtesy of the Watson family)

I bid goodbye to the Watson/Saltonstall clans and agreed to return by 9am sharp the following day.

Figure 7.8: The Watson Family
Front Row: Hoyt, Anne, Reverend Jacob
2nd Row: Lea, Doug, Molly
(Photo courtesy of the Watson family)

Back in Westport, over dinner at the fund raiser, I reported the day's events to my extended family and friends. They took it all in with amazement.

As we were walking back to our cars, my daughter Abby pulled me aside.

"Hey dad." "Any chance that I could tag along with you tomorrow? "This sounds like one of those '**Buckrammer** moments' and I'd love to be a part of it."

She needn't have asked.

The following day dawned sunny and blue; perfect for sailing. We left Westport at 8:00am and by 8:45am were knocking on the Watson's front door.

Anne's smiling face greeted us.

"Sailing anyone?' I piped.

"See you at the dock," Anne shot back.

The whole family met Abby and me at the float. I introduced my daughter to the crowd

Abby seemed amused and impressed that so many had such interest in the old bucket.

Hoyt, Anne, Kathie, and Josephine asked permission to board and climbed into the cockpit. As Hoyt's son, Reverend Jacob, mounted the gunwale, Kathie grabbed his arm.

"Sorry Jacob,' she politely commanded, "This cruise is strictly for the grown-ups." Jacob looked a tad surprised but quickly recovered. (Lea Watson received a special dispensation, however, and was allowed to board)

"OK, I'll find a spot on the photo boat," he pouted.

Abby and I had earlier planned that we would take the group on a little sail around the harbor. However, when we broadcast this plan, the passengers would have none of it.

Kathie was the most outspoken.

"Mr. Conway," she scolded, "You and we have not come all of this way for a harbor tour. It's Buzzard's Bay that we have our eye set for and Buzzard's Bay it will be."

Abby and I looked at one another a bit wide-eyed and chuckled.

"OK gang, Buzzard's Bay it is." I agreed.

We cast off and motored out by the Beverly Yacht Club and past Ram Island, retracing

Figure 7.9: Buckrammer and crew enroute to Buzzard's Bay
(Photo Courtesy of the Watson family)

the path I had taken while inbound the previous day and headed into outer Sippican Harbor and Buzzard's Bay.

The weather was picture perfect with a fresh southwest wind of 10 to 15 knots or so.

I turned the helm over to Hoyt and asked him to come into the wind, which he did.

Quickly, Abby released the sail ties and the horse line, loosened the main sheet and handed it to Anne. I took a position behind the halyards and on Hoyt's signal, hoisted the gaff boom, unfurled **Buckrammer**'s main and cleated off the lines.

"Don't forget the topping lift," Hoyt commanded and Abby obliged by slackening it off.

With that Hoyt came about, the great sail filled to capacity and **Buckrammer** leapt out into Buzzard's Bay.

Figure 7.10: Hoyt and Anne take command once again
(Photo Courtesy of the Watson family)

For the next few hours, the Watsons and Kathie relived the fun of sailing the catboat that they considered an old-timer back in the 1930's. Abby and I were impressed at how effortlessly they put the old bucket through her paces.

"Comes back like riding a bicycle," Kathie remarked.

All the while the rest of the Watsons shadowed us in the family motorboats snapping photos as we cruised along.

Jacob later remarked that he could see the smiles on his parent's faces from a mile away.

Abby and I basked in the glow of those smiles up close and personal.

A little past noon Hoyt announced that lunch was getting cold back at the house so we came about one last time, furled the sail and headed in under outboard power.

A round of applause greeted us as we docked the boat at Watson float. The 50 and 60-something years old "kids" helped the grown-ups out and we all headed towards the chowder and sandwiches.

Figure 7.11: Buckrammer unfurls her rig in Buzzard's Bay
(Photo Courtesy of the Watson family)

After lunch Hoyt presented Abby and me with two handmade accessories for our boats.

The first was a magnificently spliced painter terminated with a hefty bronze snap hook.

Hoyt beamed, "Just a little something to replace what the sea claimed from Splinter on your journey here."

The second item was a three-stranded turk's-head, a tour-de-force of marlinspike work braided by Hoyt the evening before.

Figure 7.12: Hoyt and Kathie could not stop smiling
(Photo Courtesy of the Watson family)

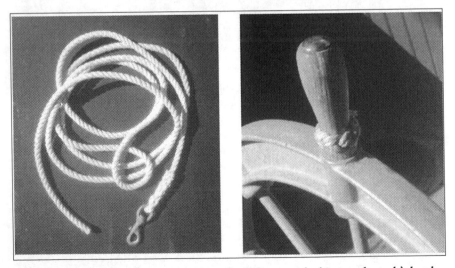

Figure 7.13: Hoyt's gifts; A new painter for Splinter and a king-spoke turk's head

"I noticed that the king-spoke on your ship's wheel was missing an indicator. So squeeze this down over its handle, snug it up tight, trim off the excess and you'll always know when Josephine's, er, I mean **Buckrammer**'s rudder is centered."

Later that afternoon, Abby and I sadly bid adieu to all, undocked **Buckrammer** and headed back towards Westport. The dock was once again filled to capacity with hand wavers who continued to do so until we turned out of sight.

Abby gave me a little hug.

"What's that for?" I asked.

"Oh nothing," she smiled. "Nothing."

Figure 7.14: The author and his oldest daughter, Abby, head back to Westport
(Photo courtesy of the Watson family

In Memoriam

Katharyn Saltonstall (Moore) passed away just shy of her 94th birthday in February of 2006. A heartwarming eulogy for her can be found in the Spring 2006 edition of **The Exeter Bulletin** at:

(http://www.exeter.edu/documents/Exeter Bulletin/ SP06 People Who Make a Difference.pdf

L.Hoyt Watson crossed the bar in October of 2011. He was 93 years young. An equally wonderful eulogy for Mr. Watson can be found on the Wood's Hole Oceanographic site.

(http://www.whoi.edu/page.do?pid=10934&tid=282&cid=118932 &ct=163)

Anne Watson died in Marion, MA on October 15, 2013. She was also 93 years old. Her obiituary and a remarkable eulogy can be found at:

(http://www.legacy.com/obituaries/bostonglobe/obituary. aspx?pid=167495138)

CHAPTER 8

SEARCH FOR THE ORCA

"I can't believe we're actually doing this," I commented as Ned passed me the last load of provisions.

He shot back, "I know, dad, we've been talking about this for how long?" "Gawd."

We both shook our heads, climbed aboard **Buckrammer** and cast off. . . . Menemsha bound and with the needles of our respective anticipation meters pegged to the max.

For years we had planned an expedition to Menemsha Bight, the western-most port-of-call on Martha's Vineyard and a mere 16 miles from our home port of Westport Point, MA. Yet we had been thwarted at every turn by Evils ranging from bad weather to mechanical problems with our old catboat. For example, the previous year we had literally been within sight of the place (on the distant horizon) only to have a potentially deadly squall line suddenly develop that caused us to race to the harbor of refuge on Cuttyhunk Island. The year before that, while under way, we experienced simultaneous engine failure of both Red, Jr., our antique diesel engine and of our back-up outboard motor . . . and we were reluctant to cross Vineyard Sound without the safety of emergency propulsion.

Unfavorable conditions throughout most of the summer continued to frustrate attempts at an expedition. But all lights went "green" on August 23rd. The winds were perfect, the seas calm, the currents in Buzzard's Bay and Vineyard Sound favorable and, perhaps most importantly, the boat was running like the proverbial watch.

This alignment of factors could not have occurred at a better moment. On September 2nd, my son was set to marry Gabriela Doger de Speville, the woman of his dreams and a fair Spanish maiden, in Madrid, Spain. So, if we could actually pull this Menemsha trip off, it would serve as our proverbial, last, father-son, pre-wedding bonding experience.

Amazingly, the four-hour trip went without incident. (!) Lightning did not strike, whirlpools did not open, all boating systems remained "GO" and schools of Great White sharks failed to attack.

All of which brings me to the REAL purpose of our Menemsha trek, *THE JAWS BOAT.*

Way back in 1975 a virtually unknown, 26 year-old director named Stephen Spielberg decided to shoot the movie version of the Peter Benchley best seller, Jaws, on Martha's Vineyard. In the film, Menemsha served as the home for the cantankerous shark-hunter Quint and his run-down shark-hunting boat, the ORCA. A good portion of the film was shot in and around the waters of The Bight.

Upon completion of the shooting, many of the props, gadgets and other movie-making paraphernalia were left on the beach and in the dunes that border the little creek that leads into Menemsha Pond. The most significant of these items, legend had it, was the ORCA itself.

The boat, a real but tired old fishing vessel, had been modified by the special effects people so that it could float or sink on command. It had dozens of air hoses running into floatation tanks which could be flooded or "blown" much like the ballast tanks on a submarine.

Filming done, the whole contraption was (supposedly) run aground in the Menemsha guzzle where it, in theory at least, remained to the present day.

Thus, ORCA was the object of our quest. Did she really exist? If so, where was she located? Was she lying at the bottom of the Menemsha guzzle?

Buried under the shifting sands of the dunes? Rotted away into dust? There was only one way to find out and we were determined to do so.

Figure 8.1: Satellite view of Menemsha Harbor
(Google Earth)

"Ned . . . There's the Mememsha breakwater," I motioned. "Can you hail the Harbormaster and see if he has any dock space available?"

Ned did so and, much to our delight, the Harbormaster replied that we could have two hours of free dockage on the quay right in front of his offices . . . a choice location.

We had built up quite an appetite and thirst on the crossing from Westport and looked forward to enjoying lunch in one of Menemsha's many seafood restaurants.

"Don't look now, Dad, but I think we're under attack." Ned grabbed my head and turned it around.

About 30 feet off of our stern roared a machine-gun laden, stealth-black gunboat crammed with camo-wearing soldier/sailors. The damn thing looking like a refugee from a Star Wars movie. The spooky craft quickly passed our starboard quarter and headed further up into the inlet.

Still in one piece, we turned into the inner harbor towards the docks.

As we pulled parallel to the jetty, one of the assistant harbormasters greeted us and offered to help with the docking lines.

"She's a beut! How old?, he asked?

We gladly reported that **BUCKRAMMER** was a 1908 Charles Crosby catboat.

"Hmmm. That makes her over 103 years young. Amazing," he said while shaking his head.

I asked, "What's up with the gunboat?"

"Oh that," he replied. "President Obama is vacationing on the island this week and a whole lot of special security forces have shown up. Just don't bother those Navy Seals and they won't bother you." With that he gave us a thumbs up and said, "OK boys, you've got two hours. Have fun."

We secured **BUCKRAMMER**'s doghouse roof, closed and locked her louver doors and headed south along the pier towards the noon-time smell of fried food.

Menemsha could be right out of Central Casting itself. It harbors a fleet of commercial fishing boats (many of which look just like Quint's ORCA), an active Coast Guard base, and a curious blend of fish markets, general stores, restaurants, antique shops and tourist traps. Boat styles range from mega-yachts to, well, military attack craft and everything in between. One of the more curious objects is the bicycle ferry that runs from "mainland" Menemsha to the Aquinnah dunes. These dunes ultimately build up to become the multi-colored clay cliffs of Gay Head light. Wild!

Figure 8.2: Menemsha today looks much like it did in the movies Jaws

My youngest daughter, Caroline, had spent a summer on the island as an assistant curator for the Martha's Vineyard Museum in Edgartown. She used her off-time to explore and became quite an expert on the place. In advance of our trip she provided a personal guide to the Menemsha scene and recommended a few "must sees." Ned and I approached one of these now, The Bite, a come-as-you-are classic clam shack servings all kinds of seafood . . . as long as it's cooked in deep fat. YES!

We ordered fish and chips, pulled a few Cokes from the vending machine, commandeered a picnic table while our food cooked and people watched.

From the large number of pedestrians, bicyclers, cars and jitneys (a fleet of MV Transportation Authority buses can bring you anywhere on the island for a nominal fee), it became clear that the high season was in full bloom on the island.

"Fish up fer two," the matre'd barked.

Ned ran to the pick-up window and grabbed lunch for the both of us.

There' something about fried haddock that does a soul good (too bad it does the heart and every other organ not so good).

As we picked the last morsels of fish and fries from the plates, Ned asked, "OK Dad, it being nearly one o'clock, what's the plan?"

"Let's head over to the Coast Guard dock," I suggested. "From that vantage point we can eyeball the channel as it heads up towards the pond and observe how other boats are navigating the thing. This will save a lot of trial and error time as we made our way along.

"Sounds like a plan," Ned replied. We dropped our cans and waste paper into the recycling bins and hiked towards the government wharves.

On July 12, 2010, a massive fire destroyed much of the waterfront portion of the Menemsha Coast Guard base. The docks had subsequently been rebuilt and most of the functionality of the station restored. The base lies along the western edge of the shallow creek (guzzle) that connects Menemsha Harbor to Menemsha Pond. (inland and to the south) So, as I explained to Ned, it served as a perfect spot to scout the channel.

As on most of Cape Cod and the Islands, ever-shifting sands made most navigation charts (or GPS systems) almost useless. Locations that held deep water last month or even last week could now be high and dry at low tide. So local knowledge was mandatory, ergo our need to examine the channel up close.

For our ORCA quest, the Coast Guard base offered one other, potentially significant benefit.

In conducting our wreck research we ran across a photo posted to the website of the Boston-based ABC-TV affiliate, WCVB-Channel 5. (www. thebostonchannel.com) The photo, shot by someone named G.Parkhurst, reveals the remains of a large boat on the distant shore across from the scene of the fire. The posting includes the caption:

"Jaws Wreck Outlasts Menemsha Pier"

"35 years after the filming of "Jaws", the wreck of the Orca still rests on the beach while across the channel firefighters battle to save the commercial fishing pier she sailed from"

Figure 8.3: News photo showing the Orca wreck (left) in sight of the CG pier fire
(Source: G.Parkhurst/The Boston Channel)

Assuming Parkhurst was correct, this narrowed the area of our search considerably. (sic!) With a tad of math, we could estimate the distance from the Coast Guard base to the wreck . . . a perfect place to begin (and hopefully end) our search. Further, with a little luck, we might be able to spot the wreck from the Coast Guard dock itself . . . for the photo clearly shows that a portion of the wreck remained above water at some point of tide.

Our short hike to the base brought us past a number of the other "must see" sites listed in Caroline's guide.

Anxious to scout the creek and to begin our search (and get back to the **Buckrammer** before the two-hour clock ran out) we passed by most of these including the N-Street general store and (painfully) the N-Street ice cream shop.

Rushed as we were, there was one shop I could not resist was the No Name Nautical Junque Emporium. Located on Basin Road, the shop sells all manner of new and used marine goods. I was especially interested in old, bronze hardware suitable for use on my floating woodpile. Long story short, Ned and I had an all too brief but grand time in the place and walked away with a shipwreck map of Buzzard's Bay, long out of print, that I had sought for decades ($10 including mailing tube!) and a few bronze hatch hinges ($5 each).

Distractions behind us, we found the government pier and sighted out across the guzzle.

There in the distance, on the edge of our vision, lay what appeared to be the remains of . . . something.

"Blast! I wish we had brought a pair of binoculars," I groaned.

Ned piped in, "Dad, that's the least of our worries. Check out the action in this channel."

I refocused and observed a swirling mini-malestrom of water flooding into and around dozens of sandbars and rocks . . . the Menemsha creek.

"Hmmm. Piloting **Buckrammer** through this mess will be a bit challenging, eh?"

Ned pursed his lips and winced.

Then he looked into my eyes and brightened . . . "Let's go for it, shall we? What could possibly go wrong?"

With that we both had a good laugh and headed back to the boat.

The assistant harbormaster once again appeared and helped us cast off.

"Don't do anything I wouldn't do, eh!?," he commanded as we fired up the engine and pulled away.

From our reconnoiter we decided to follow a course that would take us at first close to the Coast Guard pier. At the end of the pier we would turn to starboard and aim for a red num buoy that seemed to mark the channel. There were no more buoys from that point on. So Ned went forward and stood on the bitter end of the bowsprit. From this perch he could see the bottom and give a bit of advanced warning of sandbars, rocks or other obstructions. We hoped that a local boat would come along for us to follow, but no such luck. We were on our own.

The current carried us along at a pretty good clip and I had to put the engine into reverse to slow us down. The tide was incoming so, in theory, if we ran aground the rising tide would refloat the boat soon enough. With Ned's experienced eye and using hand signals that we had developed over the years, we slowly picked our way along. **Buckrammer** draws about two feet of water with her board up. I had set the depth sounder to honk an alarm if our depth reached three feet and kept a sharp eye and ear on the gadget.

Slowly we advanced toward the junk pile observed from the shore. Was this the ORCA?

The closer we got the more and more it looked like the remains of a fairly large, wooden fishing boat. Clearly this was worth investigating.

About 500 yards before reaching the wreck site, the channel forked in two directions. The right fork would bring us right next to the wreck but it looked way too shallow. So we decided to take the left fork.

I explained to Ned, "When we get across from the wreck let's see if we can anchor." Then we can row over to the remains in the dinghy."

Just as Ned was about to agree, he yelled out, "Hard reverse. Rocks dead ahead."

I pushed Red, Jr.'s throttle full speed astern, with a shudder, **Buckrammer** came to a stop and then slowly began to back up.

"I hate to say it dad", Ned warned, But this channel seems to be a dead end. We need to turn around and figure another way in."

I agreed and swung the wheel hard-a-lee.

Soon we were back to the Red Nun buoy.

"Shall we try the right channel?" I asked

"Sure!", Ned chirped. "What could possibly go wrong?"

I swung the wheel hard to port and **Buckrammer** entered the right fork channel.

Almost immediately the depth sounder alarm went off and my heart sank.

Ned yelled "Keep going straight dad, I see plenty of water just up ahead."

With the alarm going crazy, we pushed on.

Ned was right!

Thirty seconds later we had 10 feet of water under our skeg and two minutes after that found ourselves anchored within a few feet of the ship wreck.

But was she the ORCA?

We set a stern anchor to prevent the boat from swinging should the current turn, then climbed into the Splinter and rowed ashore.

We had copies of photos taken of the boat in 1975 as well as her overall measurements and used these to compare against the shipwreck lying semi-submerged before us.

Figure 8.4: The wreck of the Orca as she appeared on our day of discovery (2011)

Although most of the structure ORCA was long gone, of what remained, everything seemed to match. She was the correct length and width and she had hatch hole in all of the right places. However the most telltale confirmation came from her modifications for the movie. Dozens of hoses laid on, under or next to the wreck. Some of these ran back into the dunes into a badly rusted manifold. Neither Ned nor I could imagine any possible use for these except to pump air or water into or out of the boat.

With a bit of a smile, Ned looked up and said, "Dad . . . I think we have our girl and at the risk of sounding GWBush-ian, *Miission Accomplished.*"

We high fived, had a good laugh and spent the 30 minutes or so examining the relic and taking photos.

Just about then the current went slack indicating a change in direction.

"Guess it's time to head back, eh?" I moaned . . . Ned agreed.

We rowed back to **Buckrammer**, secured Splinter to a stern cleat. fired up the engine and headed out.

In a few short weeks a new chapter would open in both of our lives; Ned as a freshly minted husband ; me with a new, wonderful daughter-in-law and all of us with an infinite number of future adventures ahead.

Figure 8.5: Aerial view reveals many of the Jaws movie props left behind.
(Google Earth)

CHAPTER 9

A BIRTHDAY PARTY FOR THE AGES

"The 'ayes' have it, John," Eric Peterson confirmed. "You and the skippers will be the keynote speakers at our next Annual Meeting. Break a leg."

A few minutes earlier, I had made a presentation to the Steering Committee of the Catboat Association (CBA). In it I explained that 2008 was **Buckrammer's** 100th birthday and it seemed only proper that the CBA salute this milestone in some manner. To this end, I proposed to gather, for the February Annual Meeting's Keynote Presentation, all of the old catboat's surviving, former owner/captains for a live panel discussion of tales concerning the old bucket. President Peterson and the Steering Committee quickly voted to accept the offer.

Now all I had to do was produce the darn thing.

We had about three months to get our act together . . . *and I had yet to ask the potential participants if they had any interest.*

What was I thinking?

From our various adventures and misadventures with **Buckrammer**, we knew of four surviving skippers, excluding myself; L. Hoyt Watson (owner from 1932 to 1937), Tim and Clark Coggeshall (1937 to 1954) and Cal Perkins (1985 to 1993). We were also lucky enough to have Carol Crosby, the great, great grandniece of the boat's builder, Charles Crosby, as a member of the CBA's Steering Committee. After a little cajoling, I was able to convince all of these individuals to participate. (Whew!)

I envisioned a presentation broken into eight acts spanning 90 minutes (and 10 decades):

Act 1:   Introduction
Act 2:   Carol Crosby on Charles Crosby and his boatyard
Act 3:   The Hoyt Watson Years
Act 4:   The Coggeshall Decades
Act 5:   The Perkins Era
Act 6:   The Conway Years
Act 7:   A Photographic Retrospective
Act 8:   Panel Discussion

As for the title of the show? **Tales of the Buckrammer** seemed appropriate and so it would be

Well in advance of the meeting, I asked each of the participants if I could visit with them to share our mutual expectations and to gather any photos or memorabilia that they might have for us to use in the show. I explained that I was a fan of several PBS documentaries produced and directed by Ken Burns (The Civil War, Baseball, et al) and that I envisioned producing a video presentation created by "animating" still photos and film clips. The video would be narrated live by the respective presenters.

Everyone seemed to think that this might work.

Over the course of a few weekends, I met separately with Hoyt, Tim, Clark, Cal and Carol. I brought a video camera to these sessions and recorded our conversations. I figured that these videos might come in handy if bad weather, illness or some other calamity prevented any one or more of the group from appearing on the day of the presentation (you can view these videos at www.**Buckrammer**.com). I also felt that these sessions would provide all of us with a sort of "dry run" for the real show.

Each person (and, as often, their spouses) welcomed me into their homes for our trips down memory lane. Hoyt sat in his most comfortable chair with his wife Anne at his side and provided an extraordinary "core dump" of facts and figures about his experiences with the old catboat. The Coggeshalls went through the trouble of digging out all of their personal and/or family's journals, logbooks and photos and allowed me to digitally scan everything. Cal surprised me with a video tape of a PBS documentary on the poet Robert Lovell wherein **Buckrammer** was featured under sail (with Cal in period costume at the helm). Carol searched through hundreds of Crosby historical documents and uncovered seldom seen photos of her great-great uncle Charlie and his boatyard circa 1908. In one of them a catboat with **Buckrammer**'s unique lines is clearly visible. Could it be?

Figure 9.1: 100th Birthday presenters (Clockwise from Top Left) Carol Crosby, L.Hoyt Watson, Tim Coggeshall, Clark Coggeshall, Cal Perkins and the author

With all of the historical collateral in hand, all I had to do was assemble it into a storyboard, find music to accompany each act and digitize, time sync and animate the shots.

YIKES!

Fortunately, the Christmas/New Year holiday break coincided with my 'production schedule' and slowly, the birthday show began to emerge. As I got close to the "final cut" I sent DVD versions to each of the participants for review and editorial comment. I asked everyone to play the DVD a number of times to get a feel for the flow. With this they could develop their respective accompanying narrations or patter. I knew well that this was asking a lot from these kind folks but no one complained and all seemed in order.

About a week before the event, I sent a "final cut" to everyone so that they could fine-tune their respective parts. In addition, I called each to confirm that everything was in order. To a person, they confirmed that, indeed, all was.

As a show of gratitude, the Catboat Association had invited all of the skippers to participate in the entire three-day Annual Meeting at the organization's expense. The event that year was held at the Marriott Resort and Spa in Groton, Connecticut and most of the **Tales of the Buckrammer** "cast" took advantage of the offer. (Hoyt, slightly infirm, decided to pass on the all expenses weekend but would ABSOLUTELY be there on Saturday to deliver his speaking parts.)

At the Friday evening cocktail reception we took pains to introduce the Coggeshalls, Cal and Carol to one another and the Coggeshalls to the CBA leaders (Cal and Carol being well known CBA members).

Tim, his wife Luby and Clark were all amazed at the number of attendees (almost 500 that year) but neither Tim nor Clark developed butterflies . . . that was my job. (Gulp!)

The Big Day finally arrived.

As was typical, the feature would be presented in the main ballroom following lunch. The audience sat at the tables where lunch had been served; ten to a table.

The Marriott has set up two movie-theater-sized screens and speakers at the front of the room and they flanked the podium. The presentation would be controlled by a laptop computer connected to video projectors located at the rear of the ballroom. Six chairs were placed to the left of the podium and these would accommodate each of the speakers for the "Act 8" panel discussion.

Eric introduced me to the capacity crowd.

Showtime!

As shown in Figure 9.2, the presentation began with photos of **Buckrammer** through the ages set to music.

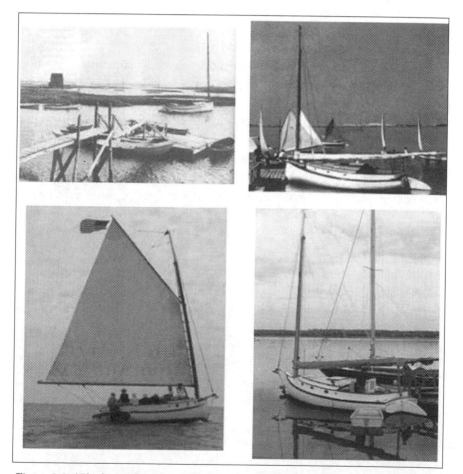

Figure 9.2: (Clockwise from Top Left) 100 Years of Buckrammer in Photos; As Ester (1908), As Pelican (1938), As Cape Girl (1984); As Buckrammer (1993)

I explained to the assembly that they were in for a rare treat. Almost 100 years of builder-owner-captains sat to my right poised to share their **Buckrammer** Tales.

And share we did.

To set the mood, I would lead each segment by reminding the audience of a few key facts of, in order, 1908, (the year of **Buckrammer**'s birth), 1932 (Watson), 1937 (Coggeshall), 1984 (Perkins), and 1993 (Conway).

For the 1908 lead-in I reported that Teddy Roosevelt was President, Ford's Model T automobile was introduced to the world, the Summer Olympics were held for the first time in London, England, the Wright Brothers introduced the first commercial version of their flying machine, Edison's Parlor phonograph was the hottest selling consumer product, Good Housekeeping was the most popular magazine, Ty Cobb the most famous ballplayer and, last but not least, **Take Me Out to the Ballgame** hit the charts as the number one song in the nation.

To put everyone in the groove, we asked the audience to stand and sing the **Ballgame** song. With the exception that some in the audience favored the Red Sox and others the Yankees, it achieved the desired effect. The audience was juiced.

Carol Crosby followed with a photo-rich description of the boatbuilding Crosby clan and then focused on Charles Crosby and his boat yard.

For the 1932 lead in I reported that Herbert Hoover reigned as our US President, Ford's Model A was the most popular car on the road, Trans Word Airiline was founded, console radios provided most of everyone's entertainment and Rudy Vallee's "Brother Can You Spare A Dime?" became the hit theme song of the Great Depression.

With the help of his son, L Hoyt Watson mounted the podium and regaled the group with tales of his exploits aboard the then Josephene S in Buzzard's Bay.

1937 was next up and highlights included FDR as president, the Ford roadster as car of the year, TWA as the principal airline, "portable" tube radios as "The Thing" and Benny Goodman as the music man of the hour.

Tim and Clark Coggeshall presented jointly and enchanted everyone with long and short tales of the "swell" boat, that the then "Pelican" provided their family until 1952.

The White House was occupied by Ronald Regan in 1984, Chrysler introduced the mini-van to the world, and Apple Computer did likewise with their MacIntosh. The Summer Olympics took place in Los Angeles, the Concorde jet flew its inaugural mission and Madonna burst on the music scene.

We handed the mike to Cal Perkins who spun his time on the podium talking about his many adventures and misadventures aboard the then Cape Girl. One of his favorites was a chance encounter with famed broadcaster Walter Cronkite aboard his sailboat Assignment. The oft broadcast expression "Walter was currently on assignment." Suddenly took on a whole, new meaning.

I wrapped up the show with a trip though 1993.

George HW Bush served as President, Ford introduced the Explorer, the B2 Stealth Bomber flew for the first time, and Enya's Orinoco Flow ("Sail away, sail away, sail away) played on every radio.

Buckrammer's birthday bash wrapped up with a 100-year-spanning photo retrospective set to music.

When finished, the audience sprang to their feet and gave **Buckrammer** and her assembled captains a five minute standing ovation.

A 100 year birthday party could not have gone any better.

Figure 9-3: The **Buckrammer** panel in a post-presentation Q&A session

(See **A Centennial Celebration** in **Appendix 2** for a behind the scenes look at this **Buckrammer** birthday party event)

CHAPTER 10

BUCKRAMMER DISMASTED

We never want to hear a noise like that ever again.

Never, ever.

The misadventure began on a high note. A weak cold front had crossed through Westport the night before and brought with it a relatively moderate northwest breeze of 10 to 15 knots with occasional gusts of 20 knots or so. This wind is ideal for moving my big old bucket of a catboat along the south coast of Massachusetts and Rhode Island and it promised to wipe out weeks of foul weather, trapped-in-the-harbor, sour sailor memories. Further, in advance of my son's wedding, many of our arriving family and friends looked forward to a few hours of sailing aboard **Buckrammer**. So the turn in the weather aligned perfectly

I phoned long-time sailing buddy, Gene Kennedy, and asked if he had interest in an afternoon of messing about. I explained that I wanted to shake out any bugs before taking a boatload of family and friends over the following days.

"What took you so long to call?" was his reply.

We left Westport's Knubble (aka Point of Rocks) behind, without incident, on a starboard tack with two reefs tied in (I tend to be cautious when first venturing out) and found only a slight chop kicked up by the offshore winds.

Gene and I debated shaking out one of the reefs but a few 20 knot puffs suggested that we should leave well enough alone. We brought the boat about (rather smartly I might say) and bore off towards Sakonnet Point about five miles distant. **Buckrammer** quickly gained speed and before long we were snoring along at five to six knots . . . just about hull speed.

Over the next few hours we tacked back forth across the waters between Sakonnet Point to the West and Gooseberry Island to the East . . . and area we locals refer to as Westport Bay. The boat performed beautifully throughout. In fact, Gene and I both commented that this had been the best day of sailing thus far this season. Smooth seas, crisp but not ferocious winds, bright sun, low humidity and the old girl dancing along just about as quickly as, well, *a cat*.

About 4:00pm we decided to make one last pass of Horseneck and Baker's Beaches then head in. The winds had shifted more West than Northwest and had died off somewhat so we decided to shake out to a single reef while underway. Gene and I have done this a hundred times. We started the engine, luffed up, accomplished the maneuver without a hitch and quickly found ourselves building momentum on a port tack, still "motor sailing."

Suddenly, and without a shred of warning, we were enveloped in the most loud, Gawd-awful sound; a cacophony of ripping, tearing, snapping twisting noises that resonated through **Buckrammer**'s hull and deck and shot physically into not only our ears but into our lungs as well. (Side note: As a board member of Boston's Franklin Park Zoo I once experienced, on a behind-the-scenes tour, the chest-resonating, paralyzing impact of a lion's roar at close range. This noise easily bested that.)

"What the Hell?" both Gene and I yelped simultaneously. It sounded as if our boat was literally being torn in half.

In a slight panic we looked about and saw **Buckrammer**'s 32-foot, telephone-pole of a mast peeling apart in a half dozen vertical splits that advanced upward and downward as we watched. The splitting sounds reverberated in the hollow, Sitka spruce spar as if it were a sounding board and echoed down through the mast step into the very bones of the Olde Girl.

THIS COULD NOT BE HAPPENING!

Gene Kennedy had the helm at the time and with uncanny speed, engine still ticking over, he brought us into the wind. I quickly let loose the throat and peak halyards (not daring to set the topping lift lest it make things worse) and rapidly brought in the sail. Even with a cockpit full of sail and boom, Gene managed to keep the boat into the wind and this allowed me to race forward with a handful of sail ties. When I got to the mast, the splits had grown such that I could have put my hand through a rear opening and out the front. (The splits would open and close as the boat rocked . . . . incredibly scary.) I tried my best to tie one, then two, then three sail ties around the failing spar Spanish windless-style in an attempt to stop the splintering. Amazingly the jury rig worked . . . and just in time as nasty, horizontal cracks had begun to develop in the weakened vertical segments.

With the mast somewhat stabilized, I shot back to the cockpit and, with Gene's help, fitted the boom crutch into the keyway and seated the boom atop it. A broadside wave undid our efforts with the boom and we had to repeat the operation but we finally secured the flailing boom/sail and could take a quick pause to assess the situation.

1. We were about one mile from the entrance to Westport Harbor.

2. The boat was under engine-powered control.

3. The mast was still secure in the mast step. The mast wedges had halted the splits at deck level

4. There was no apparent hull damage. (i.e. no leaks)

5. The mast tears had been somewhat stabilized by the sail tie "tourniquets" but the splits would open as the boat pitched in the 1 foot chop. We feared that the whole contraption could let go at any moment.

So what to do?

Gene increased engine speed and headed for the Knubble. I gathered up as many sail ties as I-could and twisted all of them, one-by-one, around the splintered mast. Slowly the splintered sections came somewhat back together. I then grabbed a spare dock line and, as best I could, parceled the mast from her deck wedges to as high as I could reach. My fear was that the mast would snap off as I did this with catastrophic consequences . . . but we got lucky and everything held.

Long story short, we made it back to our home base of Slaight's Wharf without further incident and kissed the dock a goodly number of times. We keep a number of ratcheting straps in the boat shed at Slaight's for use as hold-downs when hauling boats. I put about six of these around the mast and snugged them up tight. The mast held. Further examination (**Figure 10-1**) revealed that the mast had clearly failed in the vertical . . . much in the way a piece of bamboo splinters. The hollow mast is constructed of about eight tapered segments connected with glued, bird's mouth joinery. The glued joints held. The splits occurred in the solid wood of each segment. They ran from the deck level to within about four feet of the mast top or truck. (This is where the mast is solid not hollow). The horizontal breaks appeared on what seem to be old stress cracks repaired sometime in the boat's distant past. Needless to say, through some miracle, the mast remained upright throughout the ordeal. Perhaps this is how this type of spar was designed to fail? We welcome comments from any and all of our experts out there. One thing for certain, mast and boat got us home and, somewhere, Charles H. Crosby must be smiling. I know that Gene Kennedy and I certainly were.

Over the following days we relived the misadventure to determine what, if anything, we had done wrong to cause this failure . . . but nothing came to mind. The winds were relatively light at the time of the break (maybe 10 to 12 knots), the sail had one reef tied in and, because we were still under power, was almost luffing. Some have suggested that we were hit by lightning. If so, it was the proverbial "bolt from the blue" as the skies were clear and sunny.

We (and later that month, the insurance adjuster) concluded that perhaps, after 103 years of service, "it was just her (i.e. the mast's) time to give up the ghost and let go." Having been caught in a 35 knot gale a few years ago off of Padanaram, both Gene and I were glad she had not decided to "let go" then.

EPILOG

We received quotes from three spar-makers for a new mast (one of aluminum; two of Sitka spruce) and decided to "go metal" after learning that most of the old catboats still sailing had gone this route long ago.

The mast we chose actually had a bit of history imbedded in it.

Some years ago, Marshall Marine, builders of today's most popular fiberglass catboats, experimented with building a line of 26-footers (their largest production boat being the Marshall 22). Two or three boats were produced but were not commercial successes. Unfortunately, MM founder, Breck Marshall, had ordered ten aluminum masts in anticipation of a need for same. Current CEO, Geoff Marshall, has been selling these off as replacements "one fractured wooden mast at a time." So even though **Buckrammer** now sports a "modern stick" (faux-painted to look like wood), the stick does contain a bit of catboat history within its metallic innards.

Figure 10.1: Buckrammer with numerous clamps holding her mast together

APPENDIX I

TIPS ON SAILING WITH KIDS . . .
. . . AND THEIR PARENTS

One of the key boating-with-kids influences in my life, my dad, John E. Conway Jr., passed away on January 29th, 2008. After his services, my two brothers and two sisters and I had a chance to reminisce on many things including how dad introduced us to and encouraged and fostered our continuing passion for boating. I thought a few of these might serve as the beginnings of a short list of our continuing "Catboat Kids" project.

To wit:

1. **Give the Kids a Boat of Their Own**: When my brothers and I were aged 8, 7 and 4 respectively, my dad bought us an 8 foot, plywood pram. (Cost: $32 in 1959). He made it clear that this would be *our* boat. He would help us learn to use it and lug it around for us but this was our boat to own, maintain and use (or abuse). He taught us how to paint (white exterior, light blue interior, varnished transom and seats); outfit (Sears' cheapest oars, oarlocks, anchor, line, and lifejackets); row (open horn locks same as Captain Hatch, my dad's boating mentor, taught him to row with) and scull (a lost art) the little vessel. Needless to say, this wonderful gift infected us with a lifelong boating bug.

2. **Teach Kids How to Fish with Minimal Gear**: My dad's favorite fishing rig was a tarred-marline, bottom-fishing dropline. (About

100 feet of pine-tar-soaked line terminated in a medium-sized hook, weighted with a 5 ounce lead sinker and wrapped around a primitive wooden frame.) He showed us how to bait the hook with a small piece of sea-clam or quahog (Dad was able to get a whole day of fishing out of a single one of these mollusks), how to jig the line to "feel" the fish and how to set the hook once you felt a "nibbler." These droplines came in two sizes, kid-size (about 4-inches square) and dad-sized (about 6-inches square). My brothers and I continue to use these primitive contraptions to this day . . . as do my own children (I keep a number of each size on **Buckrammer**). They work like a champ and provide hours of fishy entertainment. And they are VERY inexpensive.

3. **Make Safety Afloat Into a Game:** Boating can be scary, frustrating and, sometimes dangerous for young people. Fortunately for us Conways, dad had a way of turning almost every safety drill into some sort of a game. In shallow water with our pram, he showed us how to play "man-overboard" and rescue, demonstrated how to right and bail a swamped boat and even invented a submarine simulator by having us swim under the overturned pram into the air pocket trapped inside. He allowed us to "ride the rip tides" in life jackets so that we would learn how these curious currents worked, practiced drown proofing with us using dive masks and snorkels and invented dozens of other drills. Through these exercises we learned to respect the ocean but lost our fear of it. This has paid huge dividends throughout our boating lives.

4. **Keep the Trips Short and the Fun Long:** Finally, my dad was a master at gauging the "boredom time-factor" of boating adventures. Our early sailing trips (in rented or borrowed Beetle Cats or flat-bottomed skiffs) lasted just long enough for my brothers and I to constantly yearn for more. A typical "adventure" might follow a plan such as:

    - Rent the boat and load up (15 minutes)
    - Sail 30 to 45 minutes to a harbor island (perhaps dropline fish along the way)
    - Explore the island for 60 minutes or so (maybe take a swim)

- Build a fire on the beach and cook hotdogs for lunch (30 minutes)
- Sail back to the boat livery (30 to 45 minutes or so depending on the wind)
- Unload the boat (15 minutes)

In other words . . . a day-long adventure in 3 to 4 hours. Just right for kids.

As I introduced my own children to boating, I tried my best to follow dad's guidelines. (*and* added a few of my own . . . more on these another time). As a result, our family has enjoyed many wonderful years on the water. *Thanks dad*.

KIDS 'N CAT'S

Members of the Catboat Association's Steering Committee asked if I would develop a "Kid's 'N Cats session for the 2009 Annual meeting. The following words appeared in the Spring 2009 CBA Bulletin and provide a summarization of that session.—JC

The session was segmented along the lines of things you would do BEFORE, DURING and AFTER catboating with kids.

Here's a summary of each.

BEFORE

Most agreed that it is essential to involve the kids in a number of pre-trip activities. These typically focus on overall trip planning, safety and provisioning.

Trip planning involves selecting a theme for the excursion, plotting the course (one or more legs) on photocopies of the appropriate nautical charts and then developing a *checklist* of items needed to support the itinerary. (We showed how one group of kids, Emma, Jake, Connor and Grace Perron of Portland, Maine, selected a **Pirates of the Caribbean** theme and then made their own pirate garb for the trip out of old rags, newspapers, spray paint, string and feathers.) Ideally the plan is simple yet challenging. Everyone agreed that (if possible) "keeping the trips short and the fun tall" almost always leads to wonderful experiences for children and parents alike.

Figure A1-1 shows the "imaginary trip" assembled for the session. It runs from a mid-Friday afternoon through mid-Sunday afternoon and covers a total of about 5 miles. Each leg is designed to last just long enough to enchant the little rascals without causing them to ask the dreaded "are we there yet?"

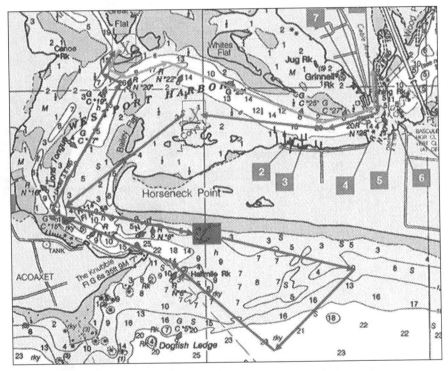

Figure A1-1: Three-day, Three-Legged Kids Adventure

Trip provisioning in the session included a visit to the supermarket for the appropriate groceries as well as the selection of equipment and other supplies. From member correspondence (and my own experience) an eclectic list of "essential items" was presented. These included:

Safety: Kid-friendly life jackets, selected by the kids themselves; SPF 45 or higher sunblock; A child-sized safety harness that clips onto a fore-stay cleat and allows kids to ride on the bow or bowsprit.

Food: A number of CBA members suggested giving each child a budget to buy their own breakfast and/or lunch food in advance of the trip. The catch was that the child had to live with whatever he or she ultimately selected. Jiffy Pop Popcorn; Aunt Jemima Complete Pancake mix (just add water); Pancake Syrup; Rod Pretzels; String Cheese; Ball Park Franks; Marshmallows; Bacon; Powered Sugar Donuts; Soda Pop, Mini-Carrots, and Juicy-Juice Juice boxes topped the list. Certain frozen foods were also mentioned, in particular, frozen French Toast Sticks. For those catboats with iceboxes, frozen food served as both a foodstuff AND a refrigerant . . . i.e. by the time the food thawed out in the ice box, it was ready to cook. In the case of the French Toast Sticks, they could be stuck on a wooden shish-kebob skewer and toasted over the open flame on the boat's stove. PAM non-stick spray was also mentioned as essential. (The ONLY way to make kid-flippable pancakes.) Adults DID buy a more healthy selection of items to round out dinner . . . there must be at least one, good kid meal per day.

Cooking: Many members suggested the inclusion of a 12", Teflon-coated griddle with raised edges. The raised edges prevent the food from rolling out of the pan unexpectedly. It was also suggested that low-cost butane or propane stoves are handy for cooking meals ether in the cockpit or on the beach and for toasting such things as unfrozen French Toast Sticks. Firewood (shrink-wrapped bundles available at supermarkets) for campfires was also suggested.

Bedding and Clothing: Polar fleece (or equivalent) blankets are popular with kids and fairly indestructible. Many suggested giving each child their own, large waterproof storage bag to use as their clothes and gear locker for the duration of the cruise. Several suggested the nylon-mesh-reinforced Coleman bag (available from Target) as a durable, low-cost option. Each kid would keep those items never intended for salt or fresh water (i.e. good clothes, books, toys, stuffed animals, etc.) in these bags. All of the wet stuff could be stored on deck or in the "wet locker." Beyond these items, all agreed that clothing should be kept to a minimum. Finally, the youth Cascade rain parka was recommended. Available for $20 from Campmor (www.campmor.com) this rain jacket has elastic sleeves and vents that prevent perspiration build-up.

Hygiene/Cleaning: Baby wipes were also a common item on many Kids 'N Cats lists. Available in any grocery store, they can be used to clean-up and disinfect all sorts of messes from infants to teens.

First Aid: Most agreed that it was best for the parents to assemble their own first aid kit from supplies readily available at any pharmacy and then store these aboard in a watertight tackle box or "ammo" box.

Miscellany: Simple musical instruments were also mentioned as favorites with children. The Horner, plastic and brass "Marine Band" harmoonica is a good, non-corroding, instrument. Others included plastic recorders, plastic or ceramic ocarinas (aka sweet potato), and slide whistles. I mentioned that a favorite aboard ***Buckrammer*** is a low-cost, plastic and brass accordion (Mini Button Accordion ~$28) available from the Lark in the Morning music shop in San Francisco (www.larkinthemorning.com) This instrument sounds like an expensive, classic marine concertina but costs a lot less and is VERY easy to play. On **Buckrammer** we also keep a three-ring binder with a collection of the lyrics of songs and shanties easy enough to play on the simple instruments (or to sing with or without instruments).

Most also agreed that a dinghy or tender was a must-have when it came to boating with kids. It allows safe (and dry) access to islands, beaches and other cool places frequented by catboats and the kids can use it all by their little selves!

Themes: As mentioned, many members wrote in urging that all kid trips involve the creation of and utilization of a theme. Themes can include exploring, deep sea diving, shell collecting, star gazing, fishing, pirates, and so on. In advance of the adventure, the children (and parents) are encouraged to read up on the subject and make sure they are outfitted appropriately . . . preferably by making their own accessories. As previously mentioned (and shown in **Figure A1-2**) the kids fabricated their own pirate costumes and torture instruments. These were used throughout the trip and were especially useful in finding the buried treasure (more later on this).

Figure A1-2: Pirates Commandeer Buckrammer

DURING

The recurring concept of "keep the trip short and the fun tall" surfaced once again. Many catboat parents explained that they had learned the painful lesson of trying to do WAY too much in an attempt to maximize the use of their catboat. With kids, more is definitely less, especially with children new to boating and sailing. So hold off on those 100 mile weekend cruises until the tykes have their sea legs and an inclination and desire to "stay the course."

Recommended activities in the DURING phase of the trip include:

o Of course . . . taking the helm of the catboat and sailing (or learning how to sail the beast.) You'd be surprised how many catboat captains did NOT think of this. A corollary to this is, of course, helping with the sailing.

o Anchoring off of an isolated beach for a morning or afternoon of sandy fun.

o Exploring small, uninhabited islands behind the barrier beaches along the coast, collecting shells. Poking into abandoned duck blinds, etc.

o Jumping off of the stern of the boat while under sail (> 1 knot or so) then grabbing onto a line trailing behind (Put a lobster buoy on the end of the line to mark its end). Make sure there's an easy way to climb back on board. Many catboats have bronze steps permanently mounted on the barndoor rudder for this purpose.

o Building a nighttime campfire on an exposed sandbar (if the local town permits this) and toasting marshmallows or popping corn over same.

o Anchoring off a sheltered beach for a morning of swimming, sandcastle building or sunbathing

o Fishing or kite flying off the stern of the boat while underway or at anchor

o Towing almost anything on a rope or string from the stern. One couple suggested building a tow-able "crayon board." You make this in advance of the trip by taking a 1 x 4 pine board, sawing two 45 degree cuts on one end (to form a point) and drilling a hole near the apex of the point. In use, the kids crayon designs all over the board. They then tie a line through the hole and toss it over. As the line nears its end, a new piece is tied on and this process continues until the board is WAY, WAY behind the boat. Cool!

○ Filling a plastic bucket or tub with seawater while underway and then letting the kids splish and splash in the water in the cockpit. Refill as needed.

○ Snorkeling, especially in tidal flats and marshes

○ Walking the plank (or bow) as previously mentioned by harnessing a child to a forestay-mounted cleat near the bow or bowsprit so that they can play "King of the World" safely while underway. (**Figure A1-3**)

Figure A1-3: "Walking the plank" (bow riding) . . . with a harness

- o The dusk or after-dark telling of ghost stories, tall tales and jokes.

- o Sing-along's using the musical instruments and lyrics sheets

- o Locating and swimming in harbor holes. Harbor holes? Almost every tidal marshland / river estuary has locations where the currents carve out small deep pools adjacent to a sand bar or mud flat. A quick scan of a chart will usually reveal this natural wonders. **Figure A1-4** shows such a "hole" in Westport (MA) Harbor. In this case the hole is 19 feet deep at low tide. Aboard **Buckrammer** we call the adjacent sandbars "jumping sandbars" because they provide a wonderful place to run and jump into the water. Better still, if you are lucky enough to swim in a hole on an outgoing tide . . . especially an afternoon outgoing tide . . . the water temperature in the hole may top 90 degrees . . . a spa by any other name. In **Figure A1-5**, the kid crew of **Buckrammer** launches themselves into the void.

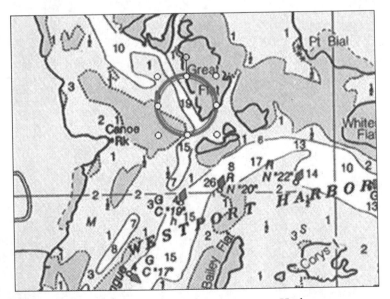

Figure A1-4: A harbor hole in Westport Harbor

Figure A1-5: Jumping into a Harbor Hole

AFTER

Finally, all agreed that the fun does not have to stop when the cruise ends. Post-cruise activities included:

○ Editing and cataloging cruise photos (or videos) then posting them to the web or emailing them to friends and relatives

○ Reading up on various cruise-appropriate topics. Books cited included:

- **Along Shore** by John Stilgoe
- The **Swallows and Amazons** series by Arthur Ransome
- **Fun Afloat** by Theresa Fort
- **Campfire Stories** by William Forgey

- **Camping with Kids** by Goldie Silverman
- **Cooking on a Stick** by Fran Lee
- **Guide to Happy Family Camping** by Tam Spires
- **The Golden Book of Camping and Camp Crafts** (out of print but available used)

o Practicing on the harmonica, or other instrument for the next cruise

o Working on theme items for the next cruise

o Issuing of cruising certificates (for guest kids). Aboard **Buckrammer** we bestow Pelican Club membership certificates (**Figure A1-6**) to anyone 12 years old or younger who has slept aboard at least one night and who has "tickled the pouch" (i.e. the expandable pouch attached to the bill) of a Pelican figurehead that we have mounted in the cabin. (In a prior life, **Buckrammer** was called Pelican and had an appropriate figurehead mounted on her bow. When we rechristened the boat we moved the figurehead into the cabin where it became the mascot of the Pelican Club)

Let It Be Known Whence and Wither By These Presents That The Ancient and Honorable:

Buckrammer

Pelican Club

Is Pleased To Welcome As A Loyal & Faithful Member:

J. Edward (Ned) Conway

Having Spent At Least One Night Aboard Said Venerable (Circa 1908!) Charles Crosby Catboat
Summer, 1994

Figure A1-6: Official Pelican Club Membership Certificate

○ Visiting catboat or boating or nautical or natural history-related people or places to build enthusiasm for our sport. In the session we showed photos of the Pelican Club members visiting with Majorie Robb, one of the last survivors of the Titanic.

SUMMARY

All in attendance agreed that catboats were made for kids and that these funky boats provide a wonderful platform for all sorts of adventures.

Figure A1-7: *Clockwise from top* - Grandaughters Lucia, Kate and Maria.
First of the next-gen Pelican clubbers.

Appendix II

Selected Barndoor Postings

For some years the Catboat Association has allowed me to post my thoughts on a variety of (mostly) catboat-related topics as **Barndoor Postings** in their wonderful quarterly magazine, the **Bulletin**. Many readers have asked if I would include a "best of" compilation of these in my sequel to **Catboat Summers**. So, for better or worse, here are a few of the ramblings that received the most (mostly positive) comments.

Noman's Land Island: No Longer Forbidden . . . Sort Of

Thanks to the writings of CBA member Jeremy Whitney (see CBA Bulletin # 120, Fall, 1999 Pp 20-28), the **Buckrammer** crew has become addicted to the pleasures of *extreme gunkholing*. Yet even Captain Whitney never dared suggest an exploration of the explosively restricted Noman's Land Island. Explosively? Yup! For years this southern-most chunk of Massachusetts was declared off limits to boating due to its use as a bombing target for Air Force and Navy fly boys. Anyone straying into the restricted zone faced arrest . . . or accidental annihilation. A few years ago an Act of Congress stopped the bombing, transferred custody to the US Fish and Wildlife Service and raised funds for an extensive cleanup (lots of unexploded ordnance). The island proper is still off limits to human kind (nature sanctuary) but the waters and beaches (to the high water mark, I'm told) are now open for exploration. Ever since we learned of the lifting of the ban, the **Buckrammer** gang has had a hankering to sail the 20 miles or so south from Westport to check out the place. Conditions this September favored an overnight expedition and we jumped at the chance. The full story of our adventure will have to wait for another **Bulletin** but can be summarized as follows: WELL WORTH THE TRIP! The view of the seldom seen south coast of Martha's Vineyard to the north, the pristine beauty of the island, and the colony of completely un-intimidated harbor seals that seem to have set up permanent residence all conspire to make this an ultimate excursion. Anyone contemplating the trip should note that we found the charts of the waters surrounding the island to be woefully inaccurate (lots of BIG ROCKS where the charts say "open water") Also, the man-made harbor on the north-west face of the island, clearly shown on the charts, does not really exist anymore (Just a rotting ruin of pilings and a discombobulated jetty). However, the "harbor" location DOES provide the best anchorage and clearest passage when sailing in from the north. Have any other members journeyed to Noman's? What do you feel about the continued restrictions? I'd love to open a dialog on this remarkable, semi-forbidden place.

Crystal Clear Sailing

The early Fall here in the Northeast *almost* redeemed the somewhat lost Summer of 2004. (See the Fall Bulletin's photos of reefed cats sailing at 45-degrees in the Padanarum Rendezvous to taste what most of our New England Summer was like). The **Buckrammer** and her crew managed to take advantage of almost every sparkling weekend until she hauled on October 6th. In the midst of this blissful month (September 18th to be exact) we sailed into one of the strangest sites encountered in our over 12 years of Buzzard's Bay catboating.

From late morning until about early afternoon that Saturday, the water turned absolutely, crystal clear to a depth of about 50 feet. By crystal clear I mean . . . *CRYSTAL* clear. **Buckrammer** floated as if suspended on an invisible string above a waterless sea. Underwater obstructions, wrecks, sandy patches, rock weed (but almost no fish!) all flew under our keel with the clarity of trees and houses passing under a hot air balloon. At one point we passed a group of scuba divers and could see them suspended about 30 feet below as if there were no water present at all! My family and I have sailed numerous times in the tropics in so-called "gin clear" waters but what we witnessed off of Westport, Gooseberry Neck and

Slocum's River exhibited at least ten times the "clearness" of our best tropical experience. At first we were "weirded out" by the event but, after a while, **Buckrammer** and Company just went with the event and enjoyed this fantasy-like situation. Amazing!

OK . . . So the question to all of you out there is . . . "What the heck did we witness?" I have talked to "experts" and conducted some on-line research without any *clear*-cut (sorry!) answers. The best explanation (from a marine biologist) is that we sailed into an extended area (in our case a MAJOR extended area) of oxygen-depleted seawater. The lack of O_2 apparently kills off the plankton and significantly clarifies the water. This phenomenon has been observed in Long Island and Block Island waters over the past few years but never in New England (as far as anyone knows). Has anyone else catboated on crystal seas? Please let us know.

Basket Case

The tight quarters common to our beloved buckets create food and gear storage challenges of a high order. A few years ago, while working in France, I noticed that many of the canal barges along the Seine solved this problem by hanging small, open-topped, reed baskets from brass hooks affixed to the cabin's "roof rafters." The baskets held everything from fruit and bread to tools and cutlery. Over the years the **Buckrammerers** have experimented with various styles of baskets and basket/hook configurations.

Conclusion? WOW! What a great idea, simple, cheap and very practical.

From our experience the best rafter-storage baskets are those constructed with one, stout handle (about 3/8ths of an inch in diameter) that runs in an arc from one side of the basket to the other. (Like the basket that Little Red Riding hood slung over her arm). A few coats of shellac or varnish will make the thing moisture and mildew resistant. For hooks, we prefer the large, honest-to-goodness brass (not brass plate but solid brass) open-eye hooks available from Jamestown Distributors (www.jamestowndistributors. com), West Marine stores and others. The broadest selection of baskets can be found at your nearest Christmas Tree Shops stores. Yard sales are also great places to obtain good, cheap baskets.

In operation, simply screw a hook into a convenient spot on a rafter. Slip the handle of the basket onto the hook and . . . Voila! Instant storage. **Buckrammer**'s cabin has about eight of the things swinging to and fro. The eccentric appearance of the little reed containers bobbing around in the cabin provides a wonderful complement to our eclectic catboat persona. At night they quietly rock back and forth above your bunk and gently direct you to the Land of Nod. Gotta get some!

Do you have any simple ideas, tips or tricks that make your catboat experience more rewarding? Let me know and we'll put 'em in ink.

Catboats in China

A few weeks ago I received an e-mail posted from Shanghai. It went something like . . . *We are a group of foreigners and Chinese that design and build "C-Cat" catboats mainly for the market in China. W e hope to bring good quality, high value catboats to the rest of the world as well. Bill Crampton is the vision guy for the C-Cat line. He just could not get the idea of cruising China in a sailboat out of his head. He first came to China in 1986 as an exchange student. He studied Mandarin and just kept going, eventually getting two Masters degrees relating to China. He has lived in China about 8 years all together in the last 15 years. His family comes from old New England roots, tracing their heritage back to John Howland, who came to America from England on the Mayflower. Family rumor has it that a sea captain ancestor visited China in the 1800s and did some trading there. There are no large Clipper ships left doing international trade now, but his family kept their sailing heritage alive.*

Woody Ives, Bills uncle, designed the C-Cat. Woody became a sailboat designer early in his career. He was one of the first foreigners to design a sailing yacht and have it built in Taiwan. Another key member of our team is New Zealander Simon Pickering who manages the Corol Marine manufacturing facility where are boats are built.

We are looking for others to join our team, as distributors and purchasers of C-Cats, and as financers of our expansion in China. Want to bring catboat sailing to the masses?

Contact us at chinacatboat@yahoo.com for more info

I corresponded with the principals and am convinced that these guys are onto something interesting. Check out their site and let me know what you think of their junk-rigged wonders. Anyone for an annual CBA meeting in Asia?

Snowdrodynamics

The Winter of 2005 here in New England entered the history books as one of the snowiest on record. South of Boston we endured 80 mile-an-hour winds and 40 inches of the white schtuff *in one storm alone!* Now, as I write this, we expect 6 more inches tonight and 12 more in a few days. Scheeesh! Nevertheless, my old, tarp-covered **Buckrammer** weathered the blows quite well . . . but not without a few curiosities.

The first curiosity occurred *around* the old bucket.

After the BIG STORM, I journeyed to Westport to make sure the 1908 woodpile had not "blewed away" as the old timers used to say. I had to literally snowshoe in to reach the boat's winter residence. There she sat, on the hard and all in order, EXCEPT for the fact that she sat surrounded by and at the bottom of a waterline-high, oval-shaped snow-drift. The ground both beneath and two-feet all around **Buckrammer** was as snow free as a beach in Summer. It was the darndest sight. After a few seconds of amazement it dawned on me that the snow had drifted around the old boat in the same way that sea water must move around her . . . sort of a three-dimensional shadow of the hydrodynamics of water flowing around the hull. VERY COOL (very cold actually).

The second curiosity occurred *under* **Buckrammer's** covers.

Once I recovered from the spectacle of the exterior snowdrodynamics, I loosened the tarp over the boat's barndoor rudder, climber the rudder-mounted steps and clambered over the transom to explore the insides. Much to my surprise, **Buckrammer's** cockpit floor contained about a dozen, randomly-spaced, miniature snow drifts (~1 foot high and wide each). Understand that **Buckrammer**'s winter canvas covers the whole boat from port keel to starboard keel and from bowsprit to tail-feathers. How in Goodness the snow got in there is beyond me . . . but it did. (It would have had to blow up under the tarp along the keel, over the coaming and into the cockpit . . . sort of like a snowy form of smoke) Amazing!

Catboat Clubhouse

A hand-written letter, anonymously sent from "an old-timer from Westport" a few weeks ago, alerted me to what may be one of the more creative uses for an old catboat. The writer reported that he (or she) had seen a "26 to 30 foot wooden catboat" situated in "a most unusual aspect" in the back yard of the historic Ashley (of Ashley's Book of Knots fame) homestead on Drift Road in Westport. I hoped in the car and drove over to the location to see the "aspect" for myself. Repeated bell ringings at the address convinced me that no one was home. So I cautiously walked around the public side of the stone wall that surrounds the property to see if I might gain sight of the home's back yard. One hundred feet or so into my investigation the "aspect" revealed herself.

There, as big as life, was a Chinese-red, ~ 26-foot, wooden, Cape Cod Catboat standing vertically on her transom-end (actually, her transom is buried in some sort of concrete slab). From my vantage point behind the wall, the boat appears to have been modified into some sort of children's clubhouse. IT WAS AWESOME! (A bit sad but . . .). I'm too much of a coward to have jumped the stone wall . . . but, I'LL BE BACK when the good folks currently occupying the Ashley home return (in the Spring?). So stay tuned. I will report *the rest of the story* as soon as I've grabbed onto it. Meanwhile . . . has anyone else seen this catboat clubhouse? Send your email comments to me.

Calling All Bargain Hunters

Few catboat people that I know would answer to the moniker of "spendthrift." In fact most are downright, skin-flinty cheap. In support of this many of you, suspecting that I might have some inside knowledge, have been emailing me inquiries as to where to buy this or that product or service. The inquiries got me to thinking . . . I bet lots of CBA members have lots of favorite places where boating bargains abound. So let's start sharing! Send me your candidates for places "where the great deals are." I'll post a few every issue.

To kick off the concept, here are two of my favorite places to either buy used or NOS marine diesel engines or parts or to have them serviced.

Used Diesel Engines and Parts

The Engine Room
Bryon Kass, Prop, 150 Mechanic St., Foxboro, MA Phone: 508-543-9068; http://www.enginecom.com/

Sort of a diesel-engine junkyard run by Wizard Kass. Bryon can find a used diesel for your new or old catboat and tinker it together for a song. My 15 HP Westerbeke cost $1000 delivered (to my boat from Kass's shop) and has been going strong ever since. Kass also provides unlimited service advice in person, by e-mail or by phone for all of his customers.

Diesel Fuel System Repairs (Fuel Pumps and/or injectors, etc)

Associated Diesel; (617) 436-2847; 66 Freeport St., Dorchester, MA 02122

This is the place where EVERY New England-located marina, engine shop and mechanic sends marine diesel fuel system parts for repair or service. They are fast, excellent and cheap. They charge you what they would charge a marina . . . who would then double or triple the fee. As a benchmark, for **Buckrammer's** pre-Kass Westerbeke, a complete fuel pump rebuild and injector-repair job (four injectors) cost me $125. I was quoted $500 for the same work at my local marina. No too shabby, eh? Associated also provides unlimited advise to customers.

Varnish Bake-Off

Varnish turned out to be one of the more popular topics of the Wooden Boat clinic at last year's Annual Meeting in Newport, RI. Several brands of "new tech" varnish were mentioned. The best of the bunch seemed to be:

Epifanes (Available at almost every boat chandler)
Sikkens-Marine Cetol (Also available everywhere)
Bristol Finish (Mail-order only. Contact them at www.bristolfinish.com)
Honey Teak (Mail-order only. Contact them at www. signaturefinish.com)

From my experience (I've tried 'em all), the three-part Signature Finish product beats everything else hands down (except for its price which is VERY HIGH). I apply three coats of the Honey Teak and then three coats of the gloss overcoat. Each coat dries in less than an hour. I finished **Buckrammer**'s transom "bright" with this schtuff over six years ago and it still looks as good as new. Guess it's not so expensive all things considered.

Night Sailing

Last July the good people at the Barnstable Yacht Club (BYC) invited **Buckrammer** to return as the "Queen of the Fleet" for the Centennial Celebration of the club's founding in 1905. (**See Chapter 5**) Seems that our venerable catboat, under the ownership of the late Tim Coggeshall and his extended family, had served as the BYC's Queen from 1937 through 1954. So it was high time she came back. The complete tale of the incredible week we spent sailing to, in/at and from Barnstable Harbor on Cape Cod is worthy of a stand alone tale. (Check the **Spring** 2006 issue of the Bulletin for *that* story). One of the more memorable experiences of the trip involved a night sail up Buzzards' Bay to Onset Harbor . . . and that's what I'd like to focus on for now.

First an aside . . . My son, Ned, in his Junior year in college, decided to convert the traditional "semester abroad" into a "semester at sea" aboard the square-rigged, Corwith Cramer with the **Sea Education Association** *(www.sea.edu) out of Woods Hole, MA. Of many experiences during those windjamming months at sea (mid-Atlantic; Sargasso Sea), among the most memorable were the night sails. With little to no light pollution to dim the starlight, the night sky revealed itself in unimaginable glory. Ever since, Ned had begged us to plan a night sail aboard* **Buckrammer** *but this mostly fell on deaf ears (my ears in particular). As interesting as the concept sounded, my mind concocted an expansive list of potential dangers that added up to nothing but trouble. Items included impacts with unseen, semi-submerged objects,*

174

encounters with commercial shipping traffic (especially tugs with barges on long cable tows), difficulty in navigation (easy to get lost in the dark, you know!) . . . and so on. This would probably still be the case, except for . . . well, that's where we once again pick up the story.

Naturally I accepted the BYC invitation (weather permitting) and began to plan things out almost immediately. With luck, the round trip could be accomplished in an extended weekend. The boat, cap and crew would leave Westport, MA early on Friday and spend most of the day sailing leisurely to Onset Bay. We would overnight in Onset then, on the change of the tide early Saturday morning, would transit the Cape Cod Canal exiting into Cape Cod Bay. From there an equally easy sail would have us in Barnstable Harbor by lunchtime. Due to favorable tides, the return on Monday (Barnstable to Westport) could be accomplished in one, long leg. Cake!

As the date approached, the Gods seemed to be with us. The forecast predicted picture perfect weather. I could take Friday and Monday as vacation days from work. My crew was ready, willing and able. The boat was running as well as she ever had.

Unfortunately, in short order, two of these four variables went "wiggy." An unexpected client meeting at the office meant that I would not be able to leave work until 2:00pm Friday . . . *at best*. Worse, unexpected schedule changes had forced all of my crew to abandon the quest. Nevertheless, I was determined to make the BYC event.

At least the boat and weather cooperated (sic).

It was under these conditions that I found myself single-handing **Buckrammer** from her Westport mooring at 5:30PM that Friday afternoon. With luck, I would be in Onset between 11:00pm and 1:00am *or so,* sailing, for *my* first time, in pitch darkness for three to five of these hours. As mentioned earlier, the details of this adventure will appear next issue. For the purposes of this **Barndoor Posting**, however, let it be said that this trip has forever and ever made me a rabid ***proponent and disciple*** of night sailing. The views were breathtaking, the sail exhilarating, the navigation simultaneously bewildering and straightforward (thanks to my trusty, pocket-sized GPS navigator). The adventures that night rekindled and refreshed all of the illogical variables that made sailing so appealing in the first place. When I pulled into Onset Harbor, somewhat north of 11:00pm and in-between two, exceptionally severe thunderstorms, I felt as if every fiber of my soul had been revitalized.

As a result of that trip, *Buckrammer* enjoyed six additional night sails throughout the remainder of the summer. (These times *with* crew) Each sail built on the joys of the previous. We had discovered a whole new dimension to catboating and regretted that we had been cautious to the point of never doing this before.

Am I along in feeling this way?

Do many members of the CBA regularly, purposefully sail at night?

Let us know. In fact, please send (email) any comments, suggestions, good/bad tales concerning your night sailing experiences and I will include them with the full-sized version of my BYC Centennial yarn next issue. Into the good night may we *all* go . . . .

Single-Handed Adventures Anyone?

In August, *Buckrammer* was invited to serve as "The Big Surprise" for the 65th wedding anniversary of Mr. and Mrs. Hoyt Watson of Marion, MA. Hoyt had owned the boat from ~1924 to 1937 and had only seen her once since. Hoyt's son, Jacob Watson, had learned of the boat's continuing existence from my book, *Catboat Summers*, and had hatched a plan that would have me sailing up to the Hoyt's waterfront residence in the middle of the 65th anniversary celebrations. This all went off without a hitch (mostly) . . . but I'm afraid that you'll also have to wait for this tale in a future Bulletin. What I'd like to relate centers around an event that took place during the trip from Westport to Marion.

I found myself once again single-handing **Buckrammer** (under power this time). A wickedly nasty southwester had built following, breaking seas to around six feet. For the five and a half tons of my old Crosby cat, these conditions were sloppy but not problematic. That is, until . . . somewhere off of New Bedford . . . ***Buckrammer*** raced down the face of a breaker as her tender, ***Splinter***, raced down the back of the wave. I heard a strange twang, turned my head and witnessed the stretching and snapping of a perfectly good piece of ¼ inch nylon painter along with the jettisoning of ***Splinter***. The dinghy had not taken on any water and just bobbed along in the breakers but it was rapidly being left behind by ***Buckrammer***. For a split second I thought, "just let it go." But the cheap Yankee in me swung the wheel around and turned the old bucket first broadside and then head-to into the sea and back towards ***Splinter***. I also cinched up my life jacket (I always wear one when single-handing) and grabbed my boathook. ***Buckrammer*** made a few head-on passes in an attempt to snatch the little boat but was thwarted each time by the sea conditions and the random movements of the dinghy. For the third pass I decided to overshoot ***Splinter*** then turn and approach her from behind. This method worked like a charm as I snagged the loose end of the painter (still attached to ***Splinter***), quickly tied it onto the bitter end of the other piece of the painter (still attached to the stern cleat) and rescued the little craft. As I continued on my way to Marion, I wondered how many other catboaters have similar, single-handing experiences to share. Please send your tales to and for publication in a future issue.

Catboat *or Catamaran?*

Since witnessing her launch in April of 2005 (not yet rigged), the new/old racing catboat, Kathleen (check her out at www.beetle.com), has been in my thoughts and I longed to see her under sail with a full press of canvas. The opportunity finally presented itself this summer during the Padanarum Rendezvous in late July.

Some friends and I had piloted my **Buckrammer** to the rendezvous' headquarters at Marshall Marine the Friday before the event. Passing through the semi-functional swivel bridge at the back of the harbor, we began to take inventory of the various member boats in attendance. While many wonderful vessels were present, Kathleen was not among them and we assumed that she would bypass the event.

The following day, as the 30+ catboats positioned themselves for the start of the race, we noticed a large, gaff-rigged boat zooming in and out of the fleet. The mystery boat so quickly moved through the squad that one of my sailing buddies, Carol Williamson, seriously asked, "Is that a gaff-rigged catamaran or what?" A quick peep through the binoculars revealed Kathleen in all of her glory. She literally made every other boat appear to be standing still. Remarkable! Needless to say, Kathleen bolted across both the start and finish lines with carefree abandon. She is a wonderful testament to the incredible design skills of C.C.Hanley and to the craftsmanship of the Beetle Company (www.beetlecat.com) and of her skipper/owner Tim Fallon. If you ever get the chance to see her underway, PLEASE, PLEASE, PLEASE take it. You owe it to yourself to witness one of the most impressive sights on the water. She is a true touchstone to our catboating past.

Authentic Schtuff

While on the subject of new/old items, I'd like to report on this summer's experiences with a range of products that fall into this category. As those of you who have visited with me on **Buckrammer** know, I'm always on the hunt for supplies that couple the look and feel of the olden days with the low-maintenance qualities of the 21st century. This past summer I experimented with a few things worthy of a quick report.

Pine-Tarred Everything: For those of us who relish the unique fragrance of Pine Tar, a new supplier has surfaced. Appropriately called the American Rope and Tar Company, this California-based enterprise (8115 River Front, Fair Oaks, CA 95628 Phone: 877-965-1800; www.tarsmell.com) manufacturers and ships everything from tarred marline and twine to hand soap and facial lotion (Yup! . . . Lotion!). All carry the unmistakable fragrance of our beloved P-T. I obtained a spool of their heavy-gauge marline and have used it for everything from securing sail grommets on mast hoops to parceling/whipping various rope ends. The stuff must have pine tar imbedded into its genetic DNA because the fragrance has now lasted two seasons while exposed to full sun and weather. Amazing! I keep the spool in **Buckrammer**'s cabin and it acts as a pine-tar deodorizer (assuming you like the smell of pine tar . . . some of my family members equate it to the smell of late Uncle Pete's medicine chest.) Anyway . . . for those of you who long for the real deal, reach out to AR&T.

Lines of Proper Color: Over the years I have experimented with replacing **Buckrammer**'s braided Dacron running rigging with more "authentic" manila or hemp-colored, synthetic three-strand line. One of the experts at Mystic Seaport had recommended a German product known as Robelon and I purchased a spool and re-rigged most of my boat. with the stuff. After only three years of summertime use, a nearly disastrous failure of my topping lift line convinced me to abandon this product. Seems that Robelon, like many poly-based lines, does not do too well in ultraviolet-rich sunlight. The fibers literally come undone. I was lamenting having to switch back to white nylon when a friend recommended a visit to R&W: The Rope Warehouse in New Bedford, MA (39 Tarkiln Place, 02745 Phone 800-260-8599; www.rwrope.com). They are a relatively new outfit specializing in all manner of commercial and pleasure boat rope and hardware. The good people there confirmed that Robelon had serious problems. As a replacement they suggested a new, tan-colored, Dacron braid guaranteed to withstand a decade or more of sunlight. I purchased a spool of their 3/8ths inch variety and replaced most of **Buckrammer**'s running rigging last spring. After a full summer of use, I have to report that I have fallen in love with this product. It is soft on the hands (much more so than three-strand poly) and it slides through **Buckrammer**'s blocks like the proverbial schtuff through a goose. Admittedly, I've only experimented with this line for a single season . . . but so far so good. I will continue to provide updates as the years continue to "blink" by ever more quickly.

Ultimate Chaffing Lubrication: The chaffing leathers on the gaff and main boom of my catboat needed replacing this summer and a few suppliers came to the rescue. The former skipper of my boat, Cal Perkins, had stated that nothing less than "elks-skin" leather would do as replacement chaffing leathers for this application. After numerous Google searches I came across Berman's Leather Outlet. BLO supplies leather in commercial quantities to everyone from sandal-smiths to saddle-makers. Fortunately, they sell scrap leather in non-commercial quantities in their showroom in South Boston. A visit there is a trip back into the 19th century. The showroom contains large bins of leather scraps (including elks skin) loosely sorted by quality and thickness. Within 15 minutes I had found a 3 by 4 foot piece (enough for 50 year's worth of chaffing gear) and for $8 it was mine. If you need leather for any form of chaffing . . . or anything else for that matter . . .

and find yourself in Boston . . . please check out BLO at 25 Melcher Street, Boston, MA 02210, Phone: 617-426-0870.

But the chaffing story is not yet finished!

Once I had replaced the leathers I needed a source of leather-suitable grease. My fear was that the new leathers would bind up as I raised or (more importantly) lowered the gaff boom. When asked to recommend a weather-resistant leather lube the staff at BLO recommended "raw lanolin." Shazzam! About three years ago, former Catboat Association President, Bob Luckraft, was giving away tubs of raw lanolin that he had somehow come into possession of. Reluctant to pass any free gift, I took a few. I slathered a generous portion of the white goo on the leather parts of **Buckrammer**'s gaff and main booms and am happy to report that they slide like a greased monkey . . . I did not have a single gaff-hang-up this summer. Next time you see Bob . . . ask him if he has an extra tub. You'll be glad you did.

A Centennial Celebration

This past summer (2007) marked the 99th year since **Buckrammer** slipped the ways at the Charles Crosby Yard in Osterville on Cape Cod. In celebration of her upcoming 100th birthday, the Catboat Association asked me to provide the keynote speech at the Annual Meeting in February of 2008. Entitled **Tales of the Buckrammer; A Centennial Celebration,** the event featured speakers, all former owner/skippers of this remarkable catboat. Presenters included Hoyt Watson, owner from 1924 to 1937, Tim and Clark Coggeshall, owners from 1937 to 1954, Cal Perkins, owner from 1985 to 1993 and yours truly. The presentation featured never before seen photos, film and video of the old bucket keyed to music (including Take Me Out to the Ballgame . . . fist released in 1908) from the appropriate era. Many have asked for details around the production. So, here they are:

Centennial Celebration: *Behind the Scenes*

Tracking the Owners: As many of you know, my relationship with this 1908 Charles Crosby catboat began with longtime CBA member Cal Perkins. Cal had discovered the boat in a bone-yard on Lake Champlain,

Vermont in the early 1980's. In 1984, he purchased "Pelican"and brought her down to Mattapoisett, MA. Included in the sale were several boxes of documents collected over the years by past owners. These ranged from maintenance records and surveys to letters of sale and decades worth of correspondence. As I understand it, Cal's interest in these papers peaked when he decided to register the boat as a Documented Vessel (as opposed to registering her with the State of Massachusetts). The documentation process apparently requires a detailed history of construction, ownership and utilization. Many of the owner's names had been gathered by other past owners and this list was included with the paperwork brought down from Vermont. However, the government required more detailed records in order to award Documentation Rights. In an attempt to locate these Cal contacted the Marine division of the National Archives. Located in Waltham, MA, (380 Trapelo Road, Waltham, MA 02452; Phone (781) 663-0144), the Archives contain many of the logbooks and papers of vessels large and small dating from the founding of the United States to the present. From these efforts, Cal was able to obtain the original fishing licenses for the boat. These licenses certified Augustus Eldridge of Chatham, MA as the original owner and Charles Crosby of Osterville, as the builder. Unfortunately, the licenses were still not enough for the Feds to approve Documentation for the boat and Cal gave up the quest.

When we purchased the restored "Pelican", now renamed "Cape Girl", from Cal in 1993 he generously included all of the papers, including poster-sized photocopies of the licenses gathered from the Archives. During the first years of ownership, my attention was, candidly, more focused on the restoration of the old vessel rather than on her history. During the winter months I would occasionally pull a box of the documents from their storage shelf in our basement and read through and sort one or two. They were interesting but I never really gave them much more than secondary attention.

My management consulting job during those years had me spending many hours on commercial airlines flying between the East and West Coasts of the US and between the US and Europe. To wile away the air time, I began writing down the accounts of our various family adventures aboard the now restored and renamed **Buckrammer**. As a lark, I submitted several of these to Bob Hicks, editor of the bi-weekly magazine **Messing**

About in Boats to see if he might have an interest in publishing one or two. Bob loved the little tales. In short order (beginning with the April 15, 1996 issue) the articles began to appear in his wonderful publication on a regular basis.

Along with purchasing the boat in 1993, I had also joined the CBA. Several **CBA Bulletin** editors (Dave Crosby and Dave Hall in particular) spied my stories in **Messing About** and asked if they could reprint them in the Bulletin. (Which they did!)

To add some historical spin to the tales, I conducted a more comprehensive review of Cal's document boxes, gleaned a few facts from the collection and folded these facts into the stories. These included tidbits about her former lives (as described in the correspondence, etc.) and former owners.

The rest, as they say, is history.

Between **Messing About In Boats** and the **CBA Bulletin** word began to spread that **Ester-Josephine S.-Pelican-Cape Girl-Buckrammer** was still afloat *and* sailing. Before long, word randomly reached both the Watson/Saltonstalls (owners from 1932 to 1937) and the Coggeshalls (owners from 1937 to 1952) and they, or their families, reached out to me to see if such a thing could actually be true. Her owners had literally tracked *her* down through my articles published about her.

Sources of Photographs and Videos; Most of the historical photographs used in the presentation were supplied by either Carol Crosby (CBA member and great, great, grand niece of Charles Crosby), by the Coggeshall family or (in the case of the world events shots) via Google Image searches. The Watson/Saltonstall family were not able to locate any photos from their period of ownership (but they will keep looking they tell me). Cal Perkin's photos were limited to a few shots of the boat under sail and a single snap of **Pelican's** figurehead which was still affixed to her bow when he located her in Vermont.

Here's a thumbnail on each source.

Carol Crosby has somehow inherited a wonderful collection of old photographs from her extended Crosby clan. For the presentation, she culled through boxes of these to find those specifically related to Charles Crosby's Osterville boatyard circa 1908. (**Buckrammer**'s launch year). She sent electronic copies to me and I easily inserted them into the show.

The Coggeshall photos were split between brothers Tim and Clarke. Both had taken numerous photos of the boat during their youth and had meticulously saved these in logbooks, diaries and photo albums. Early in January of 2007, I met Tim and Clarke at Tim's house on Cape Cod. They brought all of their photos and, over a period of a few hours, we scanned them into my laptop using a high resolution HP scanner. Once the files had been digitized, it was an easy thing to port them over to the presentation.

While Cal Perkins did not have many photos, he did have one major visual surprise in store for me. When I purchased the boat from Cal he mentioned that Public Broadcasting had produced a videotape of the boat under sail for a documentary on the life of the poet Robert Lowell. The program aired in 1988. Cal was given a copy but had misplaced it over the years. After many failed attempts at locating a new VHS copy, Cal finally succeeded in the Fall of 2007. He loaned me the VHS tape and I digitized it using a wonderful little gadget called the DVD Xpesss DX2, available from ADS-tech Corporation (www.adstech) of Cerritos, CA. The system consists of a hand-sized "black box", some cables and software. It costs about $50.00. With the box connected to a computer and the software installed, anyone can digitize videos from any source including VHS and DVD players, television sets and cable boxes. If your computer has a DVD burner, you can also produce DVD copies of the videos.

I also video taped interviews with each of the former owners. I did this as a "dry run" of what would be expected of the "lads" during the presentation . . . but I also decided to shoot the videos just in case weather or illness kept any of the former owners from attending the Annual Meeting. (We may edit these videos and post them on the new CBA web site in the near future. They are pretty remarkable if I do say so myself)

Presentation Technology: For the presentation itself, I used a software application called ProShow Gold, produced by PhotoDex Corporation (www.photodex.com) of Austin, TX. It also retails for about $50.00.

This wonderful computer program allows even a helpless klutz like "yours truly" to produce a Ken Burns quality show with "drag and drop" simplicity. The show can include still photos, videos and multiple sound tracks. Zooms, pans, fades, and a host of other special effects can be achieved with a few clicks of your computer mouse. As long as you have the photos, videos and music in digital form on your computer, ProShow can manage the rest. When finished, you can use the program to save the show as a video file on your computer or as a CD-ROM or as a DVD. The CD's can play on your computer and the DVD's can play on either your computer or on a conventional DVD player.

Once I had assembled all of the photos, video and music, it took about eight hours to assemble and edit the show. It included over 350 photographs, 6 minutes of video and 32 minutes of music. The music was downloaded from the web as licensed content. The sound track included:

Main Theme:	**The Best of John Williams**; J. Williams, Composer; Boston Pops/DG
1908	**Take Me out to the Ballgame**; The Haydn Quartet, Victor Wax
1932	**Brother Can You Spare a Dime**; Rudy Vallee; Columbia
1937	**Sing, Sing, Sing**; Benny Goodman and His Orchestra; RCA
1984	**Like a Virgin**; Madonna; Atlantic
1993	**Orinoco Flow**; Enya/Watermark; Atlantic
Interstitials	Tracks from the film **The Cowboys**; John Williams, Composer; DG

For the actual presentation we had hoped to use a standard DVD-player provided by the Marriott and connected into their video projection and sound system. Unfortunately, the hotel was not able to provide a DVD as promised. We had brought two laptop computers as back-up players.

The first, more advanced, system was not compatible with the Marriott's equipment. (We discovered this 30 minutes before the luncheon). The less sophisticated, backup computer DID work with the Marriott gear . . . but it did not have a remote control (as a DVD would have had or the first computer did have) The computer we used could only play the presentation FORWARD or PAUSE. If anything had gleeped, we would have had to start the show over from the beginning. (!) Fortunately, nothing gleeped. The frustration was that we could not follow through on our original plan to operate the show from positions on and off the stage and we were constrained to the podium and to the on-stage table. Oh well . . . that's show biz!

So there you have a little peek behind the scenes. I hope both the presentation at the Annual Meeting and this edition of Barndoor Postings motivate you to audio-visually document your own catboat . . . whether she be 100 years young or freshly minted. If you do so, please send us a copy to post on our CBA website . . . or to use at a subsequent Annual Meeting.

Thanks to the numerous members who have written or emailed their appreciation for my keynote presentation at this year's Annual Meeting in Mystic, CT. Many of you have expressed interest in what it took to assemble the show from a number of perspectives ranging from how we tracked down past owners to the technology used to assemble the production. OK . . . you asked for it and we're glad to share.

Hopefully a number of you will take inspiration from this to assemble audio-visual histories of your own catboats.

"That Little Bill "; The Unfolding Discovery of an Historic Catboat Document

As a CBA member who owns and maintains an old, wooden catboat (**Buckrammer**; Charles H. Crosby, Builder, 1908), I receive a steady stream of inquiries and correspondence from all manner of interesting people. These range from those who feel I must have some mental disability (I probably do!), to those who suffer the same, "olde" wooden boat illness and seek moral support ; from adventurous souls who wish to learn more about sailing an "olden days" gaff-rigger to individuals who have been "touched" somehow by or have crossed paths with a photo, artifact or document connected with an ancient wooden boat.

Within this latter category, about a year ago, a neighbor of mine in Westport Point, MA, Bob Kugler, reached out and asked if I had time to examine a few, catboat-related items he had unearthed.

"Absolutely!", I quickly replied.

Bob traces his roots back to the Colonial days of Massachusetts. Moreover, he and his family continue to live in the Philip L. and Kate Cory Grinnell house, a waterfront home built in 1885. Located in the historic district of Westport Point, the house sits on the bank of the Westport River. Its backyard terminates in a sturdy dock and a number of wooden boats find their home there (more on one of these boats later)

Arriving at the house, I knocked on the front door and was quickly greeted with an extended hand. "Come around to the side entrance. You'll find it a bit easier," Bob smiled.

I did so and soon found myself seated beside Bob's desk and surrounded with the memorabilia of his historic family.

Kugler pulled out a manila folder and opened it before me.

"I was going through some family files and came across these."

Four of the items were old photographs of catboats. The fifth artifact was a folded piece of very yellowed, school-house style, lined paper.

Bob explained that the photos contained images of a variety of catboats owned and operated, he believed, by his family over the decades (actually, since the 1800's). He lamented that he had only limited information about each of the boats and wondered if I knew of anyone at the CBA who could help with the identification process? I said that I did and would be glad to help.

With that, Bob picked up and carefully unfolded the yellowed paper.

"How about with this?" he inquired, handing me the faded document.

I examined the little scrap of paper and gasped; In my hand lay a handwritten, itemized, signed and dated (April 10, 1884) bill of sale from Charles H Crosby to Philip Grinnell for a 24-foot catboat.

"Oh my God," I squeaked. "This is incredible!" (**Figure A2-1**)

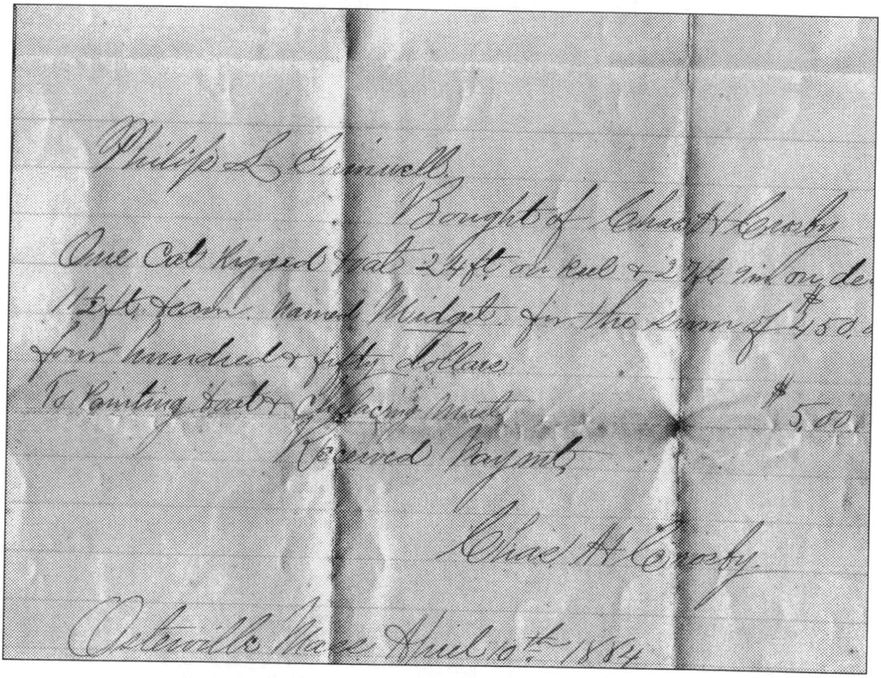

Figure A2.1: Charles Crosby Bill of Sale; c:1884

Bob managed a wry grin. "Since you own one of Charlie Crosby's boats I thought it might grab your attention."

The Bill of Sale confirmed that Philip L. Grinnell had purchased and paid for the catboat **Midget** ; Total cost? $450 (plus $5 for painting)!

For those who find it hard to read the document, I've reproduced a transcript below, misspellings and all:

> *Philip L. Grinnell.*
> *Bought of Chas. H Crosby*
> *One Cat Rigged boat 24 ft on keel & 27 ft. 9in on deck.*
> *11 ½ ft beam. Named Midget. for the sum of $450.00*
> *four hundred & fifty dollars.*
> *Fr Painting boat & chelacing mast. $5.00*
> *Received Payment*
> *Chas H Crosby*
> *Osterville, Mass April 10th, 1884*

After recovering, I asked Bob if I could make scans of both the photographs and document and he graciously allowed me to do so. I promised to send these off to the CBA's semi-resident historians for comment and pledged to send him any and all feedback. I came back with my laptop and scanner and soon had everything in digital format.

Back in my own home office, I drafted emails to the CBA experts and awaited their replies. Stan Grayson, author of numerous boating related books (**Catboats; Cape Cod Catboats; Old Marine Engines; Engines Afloat**, et al) and numerous magazine articles for **Wooden Boat** magazine and others, was first to reply.

Hi John,

Thanks for sharing these!

You'll probably be surprised to learn that, of all the items, what interests me most is that little bill of sale. I have seen one or two such bills, I think reproduced in old Bulletins. But this is relatively early.

It tells us that an engineless 24-footer painted and with the mast "chelac(ed)!" went out the shop door for $500. Twenty-six years later, a 24-footer with standard grade finish sold for $750 but that may have included an engine at about $175-$225. Taking the engine out, that would mean very little inflation in prices between 1884 and 1910.

And reference to the mast being finished with **shellac** *is interesting because I don't think I ever saw such a reference before.*

*But the shocker, if you will, is that Charles Crosby didn't write "**catboat**" on the bill. He wrote "**cat rigged boat**." I find this at once astonishing yet not altogether surprising and it speaks again to the mystery of both the term "cat rig" and "catboat." And it may mean that the term "catboat" came later.*

-Stan

Impressed that Stan could extract such insight from so little data., I decided to conduct a little detective work of my own to answer the question; "What would $450 mean to someone in 1884?"

For this I turned to the US Department of Labor Statistics for the census period 1880 to 1890.

Turns out that the average annual income during this period was $700 (!). Thus, a Crosby catboat would set the buyer back about 64% of their annual income. For fun, I used the USDLS stats for 2000 to 2010 to scale this up to today's numbers. Average US income in this period was $50,000. Applying the same percentages, a new catboat today would cost about $32,000 . . . not too far off from the cost of a Marshall 18-footer. Hmmm . . . the Crosby boat may have been a good deal even by 1884 standards.

I reported the results back to Bob and he asked that I thank Stan and the CBA for our insights. Regarding the Bill of Sale, Bob promises to take good care of that folded piece of catboat history and was happy that he could add to our trove of catboat lore.

As for the photographs . . . .

Bob believes that two of them have captured **Midget** under sail. **Figure A2-2**, shows the boat ghosting away from the western side of the Westport Point, MA town wharf (circa 1890) with owner/captain Phillip Grinnell "looking astern and whistling for a breeze."

Figure A2.2: Midget near the Westport Point, MA. Wharf.

(Photo courtesy Robert Kugler)

The second photo (**Figure A2-3**), taken somewhere off of Horseneck Beach, Westport, MA, shows Philip Grinnell relaxing at the stern quarter, accompanied by his wife Kate (Cory) Grinnell (of whale ship fame) and three nieces, (l to r) Hester Kugler (at the wheel), Lois Kugler and Amy Kugler.

Figure A2-3: Midget off of Horseneck Beach, MA
(Photo courtesy Robert Kugler)

(Our panel of catboat experts made a number of discoveries in these and the other Bob Kugler photos . . . but that tale will have to wait for another time. Stay tuned.)

EPILOG

Among the many fine wooden boats at Bob Kugler's dock or in his yard lies the 20-foot, 1903 Daniel Crosby catboat, **Storm King**. (**Figure A2-4**)

Figure A2-4: Daniel Crosby's Storm King (c 1903) today in Westport, MA

(Photo courtesy Robert Kugler)

As shown in the genealogy supplied by Carol Crosby, Daniel and Charles were brothers separated by about 5 years . . . Daniel being the older of the two. (**Figure A2-5**)

Figure A2-5: Daniel (l) and Charles (r) Crosby

The old cat appears to be in pristine condition (we suspect excellent maintenance over the years along with a major rebuild a few years ago.) She is powered by a classic Palmer M-60 gas engine (which *could* stand a good servicing or could be replaced with a modern, small marine Diesel.) **Storm King** was owned by a now elderly relative of Bob's, David Wadsworth, who finds her just a bit too much to manage. As a result, she has been put up for sale. I can't think of a better boat to satisfy anyone afflicted with the wooden catboat bug.

As for her moniker . . . this may have been derived from the 1902 hit song of the same name. We've been able to locate a copy of the sheet music (**Figure A2-6**)

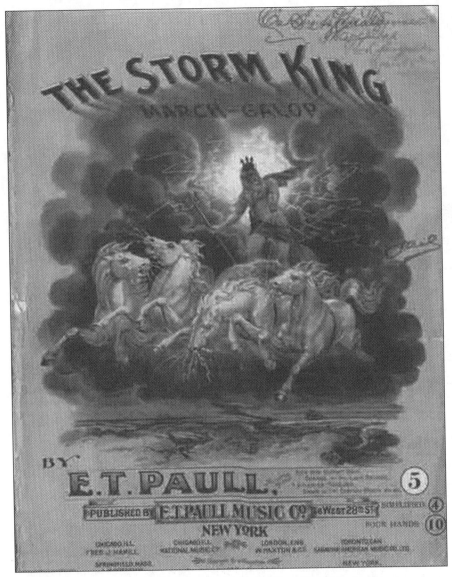

Figure A2.6: Cover of The Storm King Sheet Music

. . . and you can actually hear a recording at: **http://www.jfeenstra.com/ETPaull.htm**

(Scroll down until you see the Storm King entry and then launch the MIDI file.

So not only could you own a classic, Daniel Crosby catboat . . . *but her theme music as well. (!)* It just does not get any better.

EPILOG

As we go to press we've learned that Dan McFadden, Director of Communications at the Mystic Seaport Museum in Mystic, CT, has purchased Storm King and plans a full restoration.

Looks like Storm King may be a cat with at least a few more of her nine lives to go.